The Secret Power of Blogging

How to Promote and Market Your Business, Organization, or Cause with Free Blogs

By Bruce C. Brown

The Secret Power of Blogging:

How to Promote and Market Your Business, Organization, or Cause with Free Blogs

Copyright © 2007 by Atlantic Publishing Group, Inc.
1405 SW 6th Ave. • Ocala, Florida 34471 • 800-814-1132 • 352-622-1875–Fax
Web site: www.atlantic-pub.com • E-mail: sales@atlantic-pub.com
SAN Number: 268-1250

ISBN-13: 978-1-60138-009-8   ISBN-10: 1-60138-009-7

Library of Congress Cataloging-in-Publication Data

Brown, Bruce C. (Bruce Cameron), 1965-
  The secret power of blogging : how to promote and market your
business, organization, or cause with free blogs / Bruce Cameron Brown.
      p. cm.
  Includes bibliographical references and index.
  ISBN-13: 978-1-60138-009-8
  ISBN-10: 1-60138-009-7
  1. Blogs--Handbooks, manuals, etc. 2. Marketing--Blogs--Handbooks,
manuals, etc. 3. Public relations--Blogs--Handbooks, manuals, etc. I.
Title.

  TK5105.8884.B76 2008
  658.8'72--dc22
                              2007048764

Printed on Recycled Paper

INTERIOR DESIGN: Vickie Taylor • vtaylor@atlantic-pub.com

Printed in the United States

We recently lost our beloved pet "Bear," who was not only
our best and dearest friend but also the "Vice President of
Sunshine" here at Atlantic Publishing. He did not receive
a salary but worked tirelessly 24 hours a day to please
his parents. Bear was a rescue dog that turned around
and showered myself, my wife Sherri, his grandparents
Jean, Bob and Nancy and every person and animal he met
(maybe not rabbits) with friendship and love. He made a
lot of people smile every day.

We wanted you to know that a portion of the profits of this
book will be donated to The Humane Society of
the United States.

–Douglas & Sherri Brown

THE HUMANE SOCIETY
OF THE UNITED STATES ©

The human-animal bond is as old as human history. We cherish our animal companions for their unconditional affection and acceptance. We feel a thrill when we glimpse wild creatures in their natural habitat or in our own backyard.

Unfortunately, the human-animal bond has at times been weakened. Humans have exploited some animal species to the point of extinction.

The Humane Society of the United States makes a difference in the lives of animals here at home and worldwide. The HSUS is dedicated to creating a world where our relationship with animals is guided by compassion. We seek a truly humane society in which animals are respected for their intrinsic value, and where the human-animal bond is strong.

Want to help animals? We have plenty of suggestions. Adopt a pet from a local shelter, join The Humane Society and be a part of our work to help companion animals and wildlife. You will be funding our educational, legislative, investigative and outreach projects in the U.S. and across the globe.

Or perhaps you'd like to make a memorial donation in honor of a pet, friend or relative? You can through our Kindred Spirits program. And if you'd like to contribute in a more structured way, our Planned Giving Office has suggestions about estate planning, annuities, and even gifts of stock that avoid capital gains taxes.

Maybe you have land that you would like to preserve as a lasting habitat for wildlife. Our Wildlife Land Trust can help you. Perhaps the land you want to share is a backyard—that's enough. Our Urban Wildlife Sanctuary Program will show you how to create a habitat for your wild neighbors.

So you see, it's easy to help animals. And The HSUS is here to help.

The Humane Society of the United States
2100 L Street NW
Washington, DC 20037
202-452-1100
www.hsus.org

Dedication

This book is dedicated to the men and women of the United States Armed Forces whose courage, bravery, and dedication deliver the freedom that is taken for granted every day.

"In war there is no substitute for victory"

--General Douglas MacArthur-

"Freedom is never more than one generation away from extinction. Wedidn't pass it to our children in the bloodstream. It must be fought for, protected, and handed on for them to do the same, or one day we will spend our sunset years telling our children and our children's children what it was once like in the United States where men were free"

--President Ronald Reagan-

Chapter 3: Blogging and Your Business 47

Chapter 4: Blogging Etiquette: Learn the Rules Before You Blog... 51

Chapter 8: Blogging and Web Site Traffic 97

Chapter 9: Promoting Your Blog ... 105

Chapter 10: The Legalities of Blogging 109

Chapter 11: Introduction to RSS Feeds, Atom, and Syndication 123

Chapter 12: How to Make Money with Blogging 129

Foreword

ContentRobot

David Sifry, founder and CEO of Technorati (the recognized authority on what's happening on the World Wide Web), has been tracking the state of the blogosphere since October 2004. In his April 2007 report, he said that there are about 70 million blogs, which translates into about 120,000 new blogs each day or 1.4 new blogs every second. It took approximately 320 days to grow from 35 to 70 million blogs.

What does this mean? The blog is officially past its "proof of concept" stage and has gone beyond the realm of teenage diarists and armchair political pundits. Today, businesses of all sizes have caught on, and more and more include blogging in their marketing plans.

Launching a blog is pretty easy. There are few barriers, minimal starting costs, and lots of resources to help you get started. The benefits are many, as they provide an inexpensive way to get indexed highly in major search engines, be seen as an expert in your field, and allow visitors to spend time with your brand and learn more about you (and not a faceless company). It is also a great way to develop an online community while you get involved in valuable two-way communication with your customers and clients alike.

By blogging with customers and potential clients, small businesses can share best practices, test new products and ideas, offer superior customer services, and effectively communicate with anyone interested their offerings.

It is not too late for your small business blog to stand out among the competition, and this book offers you a detailed roadmap to get started.

Author Bruce C. Brown explains hosted blog packages, blogging platforms, writing posts, promoting your blog, and making money with your blog. Rounding out the extensive research is interviews with several professional bloggers and expert opinions to help you learn from those who have been in the trenches from the beginning.

The book, which is well-written and meticulous, is a very handy tool for those who are just thinking about developing (and maintaining) an effective blog for their business. Even if you have a limited budget and limited staff, you will love *The Secret Power of Blogging*.

Karen Jackie
Principal and Chief Architect of Ideas and Execution
ContentRobot, LLC
92 Cottage Street
East Berlin, CT 06023
Phone: 860-985-6515
Fax: 801-925-6515
E-mail: **contentrobot@contentrobot.com**
Web site: **www.contentrobot.com**

About ContentRobot

ContentRobot is a technology company committed to developing effectively designed and well-written business blogs and blog-powered Web sites. It enhances company Internet presences to build stronger brands, nurture client relationships, and enhance profitability.

The ContentRobot team is comprised of passionate technologists, designers, writers, and communicators who want to help you take your blogs to the next level.

About Karen

Karen has more than 18 years of successful writing experience and 10 years of Web expertise. She was manager and chief architect of Timex Corporation's first e-commerce web site (timex.com, launched in 1997) and an award-winning project director and account manager for two Connecticut-based Web companies.

For both corporations and small businesses alike, Karen has successfully developed a variety of brands, using both online and offline campaigns, with effective strategic planning, information architecture, copywriting, Web site production, and marketing talents.

Karen holds a master's degree in business (with a technology focus) from Rensselaer at Hartford and has earned a BA in English from the University of Connecticut.

Chapter 1

Introduction

O ver the past five years the number of blogs and the popularity of blogging has exploded across the Internet. By some estimates, blogs number in the tens of millions, with more than 100,000 added each month. My introduction to blogging was somewhat unconventional, and I am a latecomer to the world of blogging. To be fair, I have heard about blogging for years and actually believed it was little more than online discussion forums primarily used by politicians or Internet junkies with no real intrinsic value to an online business. I could not have been more wrong.

My first real exposure to blogging was while watching a TV show called *Invasion*. *Invasion* was a short-lived show about a hurricane striking southern Florida and depositing more than rain and destruction on the local residents — it was essentially an alien invasion. On the show, electrical power and communications were scarce, and the character of Dave, who was a conspiracy theorist at heart, communicated to the world through his blog, affectionately known as "Dave's Blog." Dave posted his findings and theories on his blog, and others read and discussed his discoveries of aliens and even tracked him down through his blog. Since this was my first exposure to blogging, I was curious about how it worked, what skill level it would take to start a blog, and how it could be adapted to promote a business or worthy cause.

Blogging is much more than the ramblings of politicians hoping to get elected or the endless spouting off of yet another person's opinions you probably do not care to read about anyway. Blogging is powerful stuff — and is a perfect tool to put in your arsenal of marketing techniques. It is simple, cheap, and easy to start and maintain. You do not need to be an experienced blogger, nor do you need to be a technical genius to implement blogging into your business plan or Web site.

In my previous books I covered Internet marketing, pay-per-click marketing, e-mail marketing, and Google marketing. Blog marketing is the next logical step toward building a comprehensive marketing portfolio to promote your business or cause, generate Web site traffic, increase revenue, and grow an even larger customer base.

Who Is This Book For?

This book is written for anyone who has a Web site, anyone considering developing a Web site, companies with an established online presence who wish to expand their marketing campaigns, the small business, the large business, and the sole proprietor, as well as anyone else interested in making money, increasing Web site traffic, driving revenue, and improving the financial posture of an organization. This book is designed to help you improve communication, interact with your customers, disseminate information to your customers (and potential customers), gather feedback and opinions, and collaborate with employees, customers, and the general public. As you read this book, you will quickly discover that a blog is significantly different than a Web page, newsletter, press release, or discussion bulletin board. My immediate goal is to inform, educate, and provide you with relevant ideas to immediately implement in your business, at little or no cost. This book is the ideal blogging guide for businesses or organizations with limited budgets, minimal marketing plans, and limited technical support staffs.

Why Start a Blog for Your Business, Organization, or Cause?

There are several reasons why you should consider blogs, including:

- They are inexpensive (or free).

- They are popular (everyone has one it seems).

- They are easy to establish (we will cover this in detail).

- They do not require HTML coding skills.

- You can open new channels of communication with your customers.

- You can promote your business, products, or cause for literally no cost.

- You can create buzz and promote your Web site across the Internet through trackbacks.

- Your blog is posted instantly through pinging, instead of waiting on a search engine to pick up your new content.

- You can schedule blog updates on a specific schedule, such as weekly, monthly, or even daily.

- You can use RSS feeds to push your blog updates to subscribers.

The goals for any business, organization, or cause are to increase profits, grow the customer base, and improve communications. Blogs are the perfect solution to help you achieve all these goals. While many professional bloggers and companies can help you get your blog up and running, you can easily do it yourself. We will look at a variety of blog tools and no (or low) cost options for establishing a blog on your current Web site.

You need to give some thought and planning to what your blog content will be, who will do the blog posts, what the desired goal is, and what type of material you will and will not post. Remember, blogging is a direct representation of your business, organization, or cause. Control who your bloggers are to ensure they remain professional, on topic, and relevant to your desired blog message. Blogging is a steadfast commitment; you must have the resources dedicated to regularly posting blog entries, responding to other bloggers, and ensuring that your blog is active and fresh at all times.

Before you establish your blog and start publishing content, make sure you answer the following major questions:

- Who will our bloggers be?

- Who is our target audience/reader?

- What is the content of our blog going to be?

- What are the expected results or benefits we expect to gain from establishing a blog for our business, organization, or cause?

- What content will we allow to be published freely?

- What content will we not allow to be published (i.e., propriety information, financial, personal, controversial, etc.)?

- Will our blog be public or internal to the company intranet?

- Will we have one corporate blog or multiple blogs by subject, department, or topic?

- How many resources (personnel) will we dedicate to our blog effort?

- What hours will our bloggers work or how many hours per week will we allow for them to blog?

- How will we measure our results?

- Why are we establishing a blog – what is our stated purpose or desire?

Give some serious thought to the purpose of your blog. Clearly define the intent to keep your blogs relevant and valuable to your business (often, blogs get off topic to the point of no return). Decide if you intend to promote your products, services, and personnel or publish information, stories, news, announcements, articles, etc.

You need to remember one important fact that distinguishes blogs from press releases or static content on your Web site: Blogs are conversations. Blogs are not pre-scripted, precise communications that pass through multiple levels of approval before they can be released to the public. While they follow certain established guidelines, they are essentially a conversation between your business and anyone else who cares to listen and interact. Blogs are not corporate press releases, marketing statements, corporate financial statements, or emotionless corporate memos. They are personality-based and, depending on the personality of the blogger, can be dynamic and enlightening.

Here are some blog statistics, from a 2005 survey conducted by blogads.com. The full report can be viewed at: **http://www. blogads.com/survey/2005_blog_reader_survey.html.**

- The majority of blog readers' median income is between $60,000 and $90,000.

- 75 percent of blog readers are male.

- More than 68 percent of blog readers are over 21 and 41 percent are over age 40.

- Blog readers come from every walk of life and every job category (they are not just computer geeks).

- Blog readers are Democrats, Republicans, Libertarians, Independents (and more).

- 50 percent of readers find blogs to be useful sources of news and information (this is the highest percentage of any category including newspapers, online, and radio).

- People spend about ten hours per week reading blogs.

- 75 percent read blogs for news they cannot find anywhere else.

Does My Business, Organization, or Cause Need a Blog?

Here is an example of how a major company blog directly benefited me (a customer) when all other efforts to resolve a problem failed. I had bought a laptop computer from a major computer manufacturer. I customized it and bought it directly from the company Web site. Within weeks I started having problems. Tech support was horrendous. The computer was ultimately returned for service twice and, while some problems were fixed, others appeared. I had talked with tech support for what seemed like weeks, and I had a case manager who was supposed to be dedicated to resolving my problems, and I had even written to the CEO via an e-mail link on the company site. I was left with the option of tossing the computer out the window, running over it repeatedly to release my frustration, or accepting that the company did not care a bit about customer service. Then, I happened upon a blog, which I found through a search engine written by the corporate customer satisfaction manager. As I read the blog about how much they care about customer satisfaction (a philosophy apparently not shared by the employees), I jumped right in, responded with my saga of the events surrounding my experience, and within 30 minutes I had a personal e-mail stating they would replace my laptop immediately. They bent over backwards to ship me a brand new laptop to replace my trusty old lemon. The power of the blog! I had cut through the bureaucracy to achieve resolution. With the ability to directly interact with the company through its blog, I was able to resolve my computer issues.

A blog is a powerful marketing and communication tool that is simple to implement and maintain. It can be a fun, enlightening, and exciting way to interact with others while promoting your business, products, and services. The bottom line is that a blog for your business, organization, or cause should be considered as essential as your Web site.

Okay, I Have a Blog for My Business, Organization, or Cause; Now What?

As a business or organization, you need to choose personnel who will be your bloggers. Typically business bloggers are marketing professionals since you want to promote your corporate image, products, and services. However, you should give some consideration to expanding your blogging pool to include several individuals who are well-versed in your blog standards and expectations but can add some personality, flair, and ingenuity to your blog. Keeping your blog interesting and creative will go a long way toward increasing your blog popularity and, ultimately, your blog's effectiveness.

How This Book Is Organized

Throughout this book, I cover all the areas of blogging that you need to know to be successful. In particular, I cover the following topics: blogging basics, blogging to increase profits, blogging etiquette, writing a blog, building a blog, how your Web site and your blog relate to each other, blogging and Web site traffic, blog promotion, the legalities of blogging, RSS feeds, Atom, syndication, using blogs to make money, and the future of blogging. In addition, I have included a chapter full of blogging profiles and case studies, as well as information about outsourcing. This book does not stop there – blogging professionals have also been interviewed and share their advice, tips, and suggestions with you.

I provide you with the tools and knowledge to unlock the secrets of blogging and enable you to harness the power of blogging to promote, advertise, and market your business or cause in a cost-effective way. The Internet is the ultimate marketing tool — giving you immediate access to billions of people worldwide, and blogging is the fastest way to disseminate and exchange information. After reading this book and applying its principles and techniques, you will discover the power of blogging and the immediate impact it can have on your business and/or Web site.

I provide you with all the tools, techniques, and steps you need to promote and market your business or cause through major search engines, such as Google. You will learn how to incorporate a blog into your overall Web site strategy, and you will learn about design philosophy, search engine optimization (SEO), and alternative marketing techniques.

Every topic covered in this book can be exclusively designed, implemented, and managed by you. You do not need to be a professional Web designer or hire an expensive marketing firm to start your own blog.

I designed this book for the small business or organization that does not currently have a blog, but would like to use blogging as part of a marketing plan. If you are the owner, proprietor, or manager of a traditional brick and mortar or online business, blogging can open doors you never dreamed possible. I use real-life examples, and I build a business blog to showcase the process and simplicity. Blogging can save you thousands of dollars compared to traditional marketing programs, such as flyers, postcards, and other forms of offline and online advertising. Blogging lets you do it faster, better, and for significantly less time, resources, and money.

Let us begin our journey into the world of blogging.

Chapter 2

Blog 101: Everything You Need to Know About Blogging

Before you can start designing and implementing blogs for your business, organization, or cause, you need to know and understand what a blog is, how it functions, what is does and does not do, and how it can positively affect your goals. This chapter cuts to the chase and gives you the essential facts.

There is significant value in understanding the origins, definitions, and practical applications of blogging; therefore, I created this chapter as a crash course in everything blog.

What Is a Blog?

A blog is a combination of the words Web and log. A blog is a Web site where short entries or "posts" are displayed in reverse chronological order.

Blogs can be about any subject and often discuss politics, news, world events, public opinion, food and cooking, plus there are personal blogs by celebrities, world leaders, and aspiring political candidates. If you can think of a topic, you can be assured there is a blog related to it. Personal blogs are often considered online versions of a diary or journal. Although this is a pretty good comparison, blogs are far different than a paper-based diary.

A blog uses a combination of text, graphics, images, and hyperlinks to other blogs, Web sites, Web pages, and multimedia content, such as movie or audio clips. One of the features associated with blogging is comments — which can be left by readers of the blog — thus creating a collaborative dialogue between you and potential customers, donors, or others you may wish to interact with. A blog opens the door to two-way communication between yourself and millions of people on the Internet.

Just like Dave's Blog on *Invasion*, a blog is an ongoing journal of events, news, or opinions that others can interact and respond to — creating an ongoing dialogue between the blogger and the reader. The key difference between a Web page and a blog is that the Web page is static content — you can read the page, but not interact with it — while the blog is interactive, allowing you to post responses, opinions, or other thoughts on the blog. Another major difference between static pages and blogs is that blogs can be syndicated using RSS or Atom feeds. I cover syndication in Chapter Eleven, but keep in mind that syndicated blog allow subscribers to join the blog and receive updates automatically.

If you write a blog, you are a blogger. Since there are millions of blogs, there are millions of bloggers, and that number grows every day as blogging continues to increase in popularity. The majority of blogs are personal; however, there is a growing trend for businesses and organizations to produce blogs for their company, products, and services. The exception is in news media and politics, where blogging is a part of the culture and an integral form of accepted communication.

Blogging is all about linking. On Web sites, links can help raise visibility with search engines. The same is true of blogging. Links to and from blogs to other blogs and Web sites are directly relevant to the popularity and overall visibility and ranking of blogs.

A blog is an invitation for customers to look into your company and allows you to develop trust, two-way communication, and, ultimately, increased sales.

History of the Blog

Blogging originated back in the mid 1990s. Arguably, blogging has its roots in elementary Web site functionality, which allowed Web sites to link (through HTTP hyperlinks) to other sites. In 1994, blogging pioneer Justin Hall launched Justin's Links from the Underground, which was essentially a Web site for reviews of other Web sites and a personal online journal in which he posted daily entries and updates for an ever-growing reader base. From these humble beginnings others copied and modified the format of the blog and launched the blogging revolution. In 2004, Justin Hall was referred to as "the founding father of personal blogging" by the New York Times.

Source: **http://en.wikipedia.org/wiki/Justin_Hall**

By 1997 the term "Weblog" had been coined and was commonplace terminology for Web-savvy travelers. In 1998 the first blog site list was published by Cameron Barrett on Camworld (**www. camworld.com**). By 2000, blogs had exploded in popularity, expanding beyond personal journals into the world of business, politics, and nearly every aspect of the World Wide Web.

Throughout this book you will see the term "blogosphere." The blogosphere is a collective community of all blogs throughout the

World Wide Web. Essentially the blogosphere is the compilation of all blogs, including personal, business, political, or otherwise, on all Web sites. The blogosphere is not a single, physical place or Web site; rather, it is a term coined to describe the place where all blogs live, very similar to how we use the term "Web" today.

Keep in mind the dynamic relationship of blogs within the blogosphere. What makes blogs unique is the interrelationship and links to other blogs and the interaction between the author and readers on each others' blogs. A blog is an ongoing dialogue in written format on Web pages, each a small part of the overall blogosphere.

Technorati (**www.technorati.com**) is the premier search engine for blogs. Technorati claims to be tracking more than 75 million blogs and is recognized by industry experts as the leading search engine authority on blogging. The site claims to index tens of thousands of blogs every hour, providing updated search and indexing capabilities. According to Technorati, there are more than 175,000 new blogs every day. They also state that bloggers log more than 1.6 million posts per day.

The Construction of a Blog

Many tools are available to help you write and publish blogs. Many are software programs you must purchase; however, there is also a wealth of free products to simplify the process. Before we get too far along, we need to understand how a blog is constructed.

Essentially every blog consists of the following:

- **Title** — The title of the blog. This gives the reader an idea of what the blog is about.

- **Date** — The date of the blog's most recent update or post. Remember, blogs are displayed in reverse chronological order, so the most recent post is at the top.

- **Post Title** — The title of each blog post.

- **Blog Text** — This is the actual text that each blog post consists of.

- **Blog Post Information** — This is information about the individual or business who wrote the blog (sometimes this contains contact information as well).

- **Comments** — This is an area for readers to place comments, responses, opinions, or reactions to a blog post. This is not a mandatory field; if your intent is only to push information out via your blog, you do not have to accept comments.

- **Previous Blog Posts** — This is the reverse chronological listing of previous blog posts from most recent to oldest.

- **Archived Posts** — Even the best blogs get unwieldy; it is not uncommon to archive old posts after a preset period of time.

- **Blogroll** — A list of links to other related sites.

- **Advertising** — Many advertisements are prominently featured in free blogging applications. In some cases you can generate revenue through the use of advertising, but more often third-party advertisements allow for free use of blogging software.

- **Feeds** — Feeds push blogs posts automatically to subscribers (i.e. RSS or Atom).

Our Blog Case Study

Business blogs can get expensive quickly. In addition to the basic cost, there is software support, training, maintenance, and other factors to consider. Additionally, a full-fledged blogging campaign can easily cost $100 a month. However, this book is about doing it free, and that is exactly what we are going to do.

This book was published by Atlantic Publishing Company, which is a perfect case study for blogging since they have proven that blog marketing is a powerful ally for business communications and can positively and immediately affect your bottom line. Atlantic has a unique and interesting history and is the hallmark of leadership, innovation, and entrepreneurship, overcoming overwhelming odds to become an industry leading publisher of dozens of award-winning publications.

Douglas R. Brown founded Atlantic Publishing Group Inc in 1982 in southern Florida. An experienced restaurant manager, Brown worked for the Charterhouse Restaurants chain. In the spring of 1982, a knee injury forced him to take a nine-month hiatus. During his recovery, he wrote Atlantic's first title, *The Restaurant Manager's Handbook*. Using the experience he gleaned from working with Charterhouse Restaurants, Brown created a book that gave step-by-step instructions to anyone wishing to open a restaurant. Soon after Brown published his book, he founded Atlantic as a part-time business and worked out of his Fort Lauderdale home for the next seven years.

By 1989, Atlantic became a full-time business. It was a unique entity in the market because it was one of the few publishers that specialized in how-to books for the hospitality industry and, as such, it was faced with little competition. In 1992, Atlantic relocated to Ocala, Florida, where the company prospered; however, by the mid to late 90s, it faced an obstacle that nearly bankrupted them.

In 1996, Atlantic was nearly devastated by its first real competition: **Amazon.com**. Because of the site's cheaper prices, many customers were calling to ask for ISBN numbers to find the same books on Amazon for less money. From 1996 through 1997, Atlantic experienced a 30 percent decline in sales because it was a distributor of books instead of a publisher.

By 1999, Atlantic was heavily in debt and had to shut down operations. It briefly flirted with the idea of filing Chapter 11 bankruptcy. However, Brown knew that if Atlantic began publishing its own books and using Amazon as one of its distributors, it would no longer be in competition with the company. By 2001 the company had repaid all its debts and began publishing its own books.

Currently, Atlantic uses Amazon as one of its main distributors. Branching out of the hospitality industry, it now specializes in several fields, including real estate, personal finance, entrepreneurship, human resources, banking, marketing, and management. For more information about Atlantic Publishing or for a list of available titles, visit **http://www.atlantic-pub.com**. Throughout this book, you'll see how Atlantic has embraced blogging to market new releases, engage customers, and improve the quality of its communications, as well as its product lines.

In this book,. we evaluate the free blogging options and set up our first blog, optimize it for search engine visibility, and start using the blog to promote new products, press releases, and other information. I capture every single detail of the process and include them in this book so you can easily duplicate it.

Blogs Versus Content Management Systems

Throughout this book, you will see blog software and content management system (CMS) software. They are distinctly different, although related. Blog software simply provides you with the features and functionality to create, maintain, and manage your blog. Content management systems typically have a built-in blogging module and provide significantly more features and functionality. While I will mention several full features CMS applications, this book is primarily designed to help you establish free blogs using free blog software. There are several, highly regarded content management systems on the market; I recommend you check out ExpressionEngine (http://**www. expressionengine.com**).

Understanding Pingbacks and Trackbacks

Aside from posting comments, questions, opinions, and concerns, readers can also link directly to your blog posts and recommend your blog to others. This is called trackbacks and pingbacks.

Trackbacks are a notification method between blogs. It allows a blog reader to send a notice to other that the blog might be something they would have an interest in reading. Let me give you an example:

- I publish something in my blog about my next book title.

- A reader sees this and decides to leave a comment. In addition to other blog readers seeing what he has posted, he also wants my readers to comment on his blog.

- The reader posts something on his blog and sends a trackback to my blog.

- I receive the trackback and display it on my blog, along with the link back to the blog reader's post on his blog.

- Anyone who reads his blog can follow the trackback to my blog and vice versa.

Essentially this is how blogging is different from Web sites and discussion forums. The theory is that blog readers from both blogs can read the blog posts and, ultimately, more people join in. The idea is to encourage blog readers to click on the trackback link and visit the other blog (and post comments).

The number of blog posts and trackback links can grow exponentially. The problem is that they can be spammed or spoofed easily, and there is not an authentication process to ensure that a trackback is valid — thus pingbacks.

Pingbacks, according to **http://www.hixie.ch/specs/pingback**, are "a method for Web authors to request notification when somebody links to one of their documents. Typically, Web publishing software will automatically inform the relevant parties on behalf of the user, allowing for the possibility of automatically creating links to referring documents." Let me give you an example:

- I publish something in my blog about my next book title.

- A reader sees this blog post and decides to leave a comment. In addition to any other blog readers seeing what he has posted, he also wants my readers to comment on his blog.

- The reader posts something on his blog and links back to my blog.

- The reader's blogging software automatically sends a notification to me, telling me that my blog has been linked to. My blog software automatically includes this information about the link in my blog.

Confused? Yes, they are very similar. Here are the differences:

- They use different technologies to communicate.

- Pingbacks are automated, while trackbacks are manual. A pingback automatically finds hyperlinks within a blog and tries to communicate with those URLs, whereas trackbacks require you to manually enter the trackback URL.

- Trackbacks send the comments; pingbacks do not. Trackbacks typically send only part of your comments to intrigue the reader into following the actual links to read the entire blog or blog entries.

- Pingbacks appears as links only. Trackbacks appear as links with some content/comments.

- Trackbacks can be faked, spoofed, and spammed. Pingbacks are not easily faked.

- Trackbacks provide the reader with a preview of the content on the blog, whereas pingbacks do not.

Blogging and SPAM

Just as SPAM is a huge problem for e-mail, it is also a growing problem for blogs. Essentially, there are two major categories of SPAM when dealing with blogs. They are:

- Bogus (SPAM) blogs are designed purely for spamming purposes by launching SPAM attacks through viral methods.

- Comment SPAM, in which SPAM comments are inserted into legitimate blogs.

Spam blogs are known as SPLOGS (SPAM + blog = SPLOG). According to Wikipedia.com (**http://en.wikipedia.org/wiki/ Spam_blog**), SPLOGS are "artificially created Weblog sites which the author uses to promote affiliated Web sites or to increase the search engine rankings of associated sites. The purpose of a SPLOG can be to increase the page rank or backlink portfolio of affiliate Web sites, to artificially inflate paid ad impressions from visitors, and/or use the blog as a link outlet to get new sites indexed. Spam blogs are usually a type of scraper site, where content is often either Inauthentic Text or merely stolen from other Websites. These blogs usually contain a high number of links to sites associated with the SPLOG creator which are often disreputable or otherwise useless Web sites."

Comment SPAM is simply when inappropriate, useless, or otherwise offensive comments (including trackbacks and pingbacks) are posted to a blog. They contain links to one or more Web sites, which are usually irrelevant or purely SPAM sites. Combating SPAM blog entries is time consuming, frustrating, and a growing problem. While most blog software has built-in tools to combat comment SPAM, they are not foolproof. Spammers use automated software applications, robots, auto-responders, and other techniques to disseminate SPAM throughout the blogosphere. The secret to defeating (or minimizing) SPAM in your blogs is to use the tools provided by your blog software and host. Just like with e-mail, you may not stop all content SPAM, but you can minimize it. SPAM is not a reason to quit blogging; it is, however, an annoyance you have to deal with.

Blog Software & Blog Hosting Options

To create your own blog, you need blogging software and Web hosting. Essentially, you have four choices. These are:

- **Free Blog Software with Free Blog Hosting:** This option is completely at no cost to you. The trade off? Often you must allow advertisements to be placed within or on your blog pages. These advertisements are typically obtrusive and do not generate any income for you. Also, free blogging software usually has reduced functionality compared to paid software. You may have limited features, limited access, and limited control over the design. You have no control over the domain name and will often be assigned a subdomain. However, the free blog is what this book is about. There are two outstanding, advertisement-free options that will not cost you a thing, and you can have your blog up and running in five minutes. I will show you how to use both Blogger and WordPress in Chapter Six. They both produce professional blogs, have customizable templates, are powerful, and very easy to use. Blogger even lets you switch between a hosted application and publishing directly to your Web server via FTP.

- **Free Blog Software with Paid Blog Hosting:** You pay for the domain name and/or hosting space with the hosting company, and the blog software is provided at no cost to you. This is very common with many Web hosting companies. You do not have advertising on your blog, but the software may have reduced functionality compared to commercial software. In most instances this is an acceptable option since your blog is usually hosted under your own domain name. Since your hosting company is providing the blog software, you are stuck with the brand they use; however, they take care of the installation and maintenance, which can be a headache to deal with. In some cases, you may have to pay extra for blogging features.

- **Paid Blog Software with Paid Blog Hosting:** This means you buy the full-featured software and also pay for the hosting service through a service provider. Great option if you need a very powerful blog or content management system software or your own domain name. This option is feature-rich, fully functional, and offers you complete control. However, the costs may increase as your traffic increases.

- **Paid Blog Software Hosted on Your Own Web Servers:** This means you buy the full-featured software and install and host it on your own servers (i.e., you physically own or lease the servers, not shared hosting space). Nice option if you already have Web servers.

If you have your own Web site, you can usually use your own site to host your blog, if your Web host allows you to install any required blog software. Most blog software requires MySQL support, and you may not be able to install the software onto many commercial hosting accounts. Obviously if you are your own Web service provider, you have full control to install your own blog software. Blogger is a great choice. It is hosted free on blogspot.com and, if you want, you can (with the click on a button) host it on your own Web servers via FTP, meaning there is no software to install on your Web servers.

The free options may not offer you all the functionality you desire; however, both Blogger and WordPress will meet the needs of most small businesses, organizations, or causes. Even with free blog hosting, do not forget the power of hyperlinks. You can easily establish a blog on a commercial hosting provider and link/integrate that blog into your own Web site, even though it is not physically hosted on your own Web servers or using the same URL as your company Web site. This is very common, and although it might be preferable to host under your own domain name, it is not critical. Blogger allows you to host under your domain name as part of their built-in functionality, and WordPress allows you to export your blog if you want to move it to a new domain.

Keep in mind, down the road, if you outgrow the free products, you may want to move to a new domain name. If your audience already knows the old domain name, it may be hard to move your blog without losing your audience.

Blog Software Comparison

Let us review many of the available and most popular blog software applications available.

Full-Service Blog Provider

Full-service blog providers host your blog on their servers. You don't have to download or install software. For each of these providers, visit their site for details and pricing.

- TypePad (**www.typepad.com**) is probably the most recognizable full-service blog provider. Typepad is full featured, easy to use, and an industry leader. It offers a wide variety of features, including blog templates, customized layouts, and much more.

- Blogware (**home.blogware.com**) is an enormously popular online application that is sold and hosted through retailers' Web servers. The obvious advantage to this is you can select who your blog hosting provider will be.

- Squarespace (**www.squarespace.com**) is a full-featured software package for managing Web sites and blogs. Squarespace helps you build stylish, state-of-the-art blogs. The Squarespace Journal, which can represent either a piece of your site or your entire site, is an ideal way to create a professional blog.

Independent Blog Software

There are dozens of blog software products that you can purchase, install, and customize on your server. Here are some of the best; check their sites for a list of features and pricing.

- Movable Type (**www.movabletype.com**) is very powerful and user-friendly software that is free for personal use.

- Intesync Blog Writer (**http://www.miniweb2. com/10modules/blog-writer.htm**) enables you to quickly share your ideas and thoughts by establishing a quick and professional looking blog.

- Expression Engine (**http://www.expressionengine.com**) is arguably the most powerful CMS application on the market. It is blogging software and much more. The features of ExpressionEngine are seemingly endless, and a full list is available at **http://expressionengine.com/overview/features/**. ExpressionEngine offers Web publishing, blog publishing, built-in templates, a mailing list manager, built-in search, and group and member management.

- MiniWeb 2.0 Blog (**http://www.miniweb2.com**) is a suite of products available for download and installation on your Web server.

There are dozens of other blog writing software programs you can purchase; however, this book is designed to tell you how to blog for free, so let us look at the two major players in free blogging.

Freeware Blog Software

Blogger and WordPress both offer absolutely free blogging software. Let us take a close look at each.

Blogger

Blogger (**http://www.blogger.com**) is very basic, but an effective way to start a blog quickly and easily. Blogger, which was started in 1999, was recently bought by Google, it will continue to be supported and improved upon.

Blogger uses standard templates to get you started right away without the need to learn HTML; however, Blogger also allows you to edit your blog's HTML code whenever you want. You can also use custom colors and fonts to modify the appearance of your blog.

Blogger's simple drag-and-drop system lets you easily decide exactly where your posts, profiles, archives, and other parts of your blog should live on the page. Blogger also allows you to upload photos and embed them in your blog.

Blogger Mobile lets you send photos and text straight to your blog while you are on-the-go. All you need to do is send a message to go@blogger.com from your phone.

We will use Blogger to create our own blog later in the book. You will not find a simpler free option for creating a blog. However, for business, you may wish to choose WordPress or invest in blog software that you can host on your site, such as Blog Writer.

Wordpress

WordPress (**http://www.wordpress.org**) is a free, open-source blogging application. WordPress is full featured, fairly simple to install (you need MySQL and PHP 4 support) or, if you prefer, you can have it hosted on WordPress servers for absolutely no charge. WordPress boasts outstanding features that will give you control over most aspects of your blog without being overcomplicated.

WordPress has features for user management, dynamic page generation, RSS, Atom feeds, customizable templates and themes, password protection, plug-ins to enhance functionality, scheduled postings, multi-page posts, file and picture uploads, categories, e-mail blog updates (send your posts via e-mail and have them automatically appear on your blog), and much more. In fact, it is as powerful and feature rich as most commercial blogging applications. You should install it on your existing Web servers (if they can support it) or, as an alternative, get it hosted free on WordPress servers.

Chapter 3

Blogging and Your Business

Blogging for your business opens a virtual door directly into your business. The underlying principles of blogging are a perfect fit for a customer-oriented business model in which you want to allow customers, potential customers, readers, site visitors, or fellow bloggers to engage you in two-way communications. You can promote your products, answer questions, engage customers, and give out expert advice, tips, and suggestions, plus much more. Remember, a Web site is static in nature. The content only changes when you change it. By nature, a blog is ever-morphing, as more and more dialogue is added to it.

Additionally, you can empower employees (and even outsiders) to speak on behalf of your business. This empowerment allows you to inspire creativity and ingenuity, and lets your workers become part of your management team by being the voice of the company or organization. This empowerment is powerful stuff; it lets your employees become part of your overall marketing and communication plans, and by giving your employees the power to be corporate bloggers, you open new communications channels with customers, promote your products and services, and increase both customer and employee loyalty and satisfaction.

Business Blog Communications – How Does It All Work?

For explanation purposes, let us assume that we already have a blog for our business, and today we are going to update it. Here is the process that takes place:

- Our resident corporate blogger (or anyone who blogs) writes something and publishes to our blog.

- Your blog software announces there is an update to your blog. This is critical to understand. Blog software actually pings blog search engines and news readers that you have fresh content for them to check. (The process of notifying search engines of your new content is called "pinging.") A blogging secret is to use Ping-O-Matic (**http://pingomatic. com/**) after each blog update to ensure your blog is re-indexed. Most blog software automates the ping process as well. Here are some other ping servers:

  o **http://rpc.technorati.com/rpc/ping**

  o **http://rpc.pingomatic.com/**

  o **http://api.feedster.com/ping**

  o **http://rpc.newsgator.com/**

  o **http://xping.pubsub.com/ping**

- After you ping major search engines, such as Google

(**http://blogsearch.google.com**), RSS services will index your blog and retrieve the new content. We will cover RSS feeds in a later chapter of this book, but by offering an RSS feed, people can be notified when you update your blog (this is called syndication). Please note that RSS is not the only game in town; Atom is growing in popularity and there are several other syndication formats as well.

- Another critical component to blogs is trackbacks, which we discussed in the last chapter. Whenever you discuss someone's blog (or blog post), ensure that you always include a trackback.

Business Blogging Guidelines and Recommendations

Here are some general business blogging recommendations you may wish to consider as you embark on your blog journey:

- I mentioned this previously, but give some serious thought and consideration to who your bloggers will be. You need to choose the right people, and establish ground rules and limitations for what you will and will not allow. Blogging can be emotional, so choose bloggers who are even-tempered and will not be flustered by a few negative comments. You do not want a loose cannon representing your company.

- Determine your overall goals and objectives. Blogging is dynamic (and disposable); if your blogs are not achieving your objectives, do not change your objectives — change how are you are blogging.

- Blogging is a communications tool. Your blogs need to be on topic and oriented to your business goals and objectives. If a blogger is representing your business, organization, or cause, he needs to put the interests and goals of those above his own personal feelings, thoughts, or opinions. If a blogger cannot differentiate between his personal opinions and those of the company or organization, replace him or her.

- Expect SPAM, and then you will not be surprised. You need to allow comments for your blog to realize its full potential and offer the most interaction with readers, but it will attract spam. Employ the anti-SPAM techniques your blog software has and do your best to manage the spam. Be prepared to address the resource requirements to monitor and cleanse your blog of SPAM.

- Make sure that blogging fits your overall marketing and communication plans. There is no golden rule requiring you to have a blog. While many businesses and organizations have implemented blogging successfully, there are many more that have either implemented it with no measurable benefit (because they had no objectives) or they have hurt the corporate image (because they had no ground rules or limitations on what their bloggers could do.

Chapter 4

Blogging Etiquette: Learn the Rules Before You Blog

The blogosphere has developed informal rules and behavior protocols to follow. While it might seem silly to cover blogging etiquette (because you can essentially blog however you want), it is worthwhile to review this chapter. If you do not play by the rules, your blog will lose readers.

Blogging Etiquette Advice

These blogging etiquette tidbits will keep you out of trouble and ensure that your blog is readily accepted in the blogosphere. The golden rule with blogs, especially corporate or organizational blogs, is to stay on topic, establish and follow ground rules, and apply some common sense.

- Your blog is public. It is on the Internet for anyone to read. Although you may be targeting a specific audience, everyone can read it and post comments. Your blog not only represents your business, organization, or cause, but it is your voice — make sure it is appropriate and sends the message you want it to.

- A blog is not really for you. It is for your readers. Write for the reader. You need to be captivating, interesting, and, most of all, relevant to something they are interested in.

- Expect SPAM comments. Likewise, expect negative, argumentative, and insulting comments. Some bloggers are jerks, and they thrive on spreading the gospel of hate, stupidity, and ignorance. You can edit these comments out, or you can roll with the punches and dish it right back out. While you can take some more liberties with personal blogs, when dealing with business, your options are limited. Kill them with kindness, stay relevant, stick to your ground rules, and push the company message. You will not make everyone happy all the time, so do not try. For those who just cannot give it up, ban them.

- Make sure your contribution is relevant, on topic, and adds value. It is perfectly fine to disagree with a blogger's entry, but back up your argument or opinion with facts and supporting arguments. Do not post nonsense.

- You should expect positive comments on your blog. When you get them, take the time to thank the individual.

- Update your blog on a regular basis. If you update daily, stick to that routine. If you cannot commit to that, do it weekly. Your readers will expect updates on a periodic basis. If you tell them your blog will be updated daily, but never is, they will quickly lose interest.

- On all your blogs include RSS or Atom feeds so people can subscribe and receive your blog updates automatically.

- When reproducing an article or something someone else has written, get permission.

- If you are including information from another blog or are discussing topics that are referenced on another blog, put a link to the original source.

- Make sure your links are clearly defined. Describe links that are included in your blog and where they go.

- The blogosphere is full of know-it-all, self-proclaimed masters of everything who only believe their ideas are right and all others are wrong. Again, be professional, respectful, and do not engage in an argument, especially on your business blog.

- Respond to comments. Your readers post comments for a reason: They expect a response. The whole point of a blog is dialogue; it must be two-way.

- Blogs are meant to be linked to. There is some debate about whether you should ask permission to link to other blogs. I see no reason for asking, so do not waste your time doing so.

- You should not steal Web site content and post it in your blog (unless you have permission to do so). You should not take images from a Web site and embed them in your blog. It is acceptable, however, to link to an image on another site or blog.

- Respect others' privacy. Do not make blogs personal (i.e., talk about individuals without their knowledge). There is nothing wrong with public opinion, praise, and recognition of others; however, no personal information (SSN, address, phone numbers, e-mail, etc.) should ever be revealed in a blog.

- Add blogs you read regularly to your blogroll, which is a blogger's list of his favorite blogs. Add the ones that matter to you most.

- Be open-minded. Blogs can be fun, persuasive, interactive, thought-provoking, and engaging. If you are close-minded, you are missing the point of blogging. Be open to ideas. If you do not agree, post a respectful comment with your opinions or thoughts and back them up. This is how good blogs become great.

- If you read someone else's blog should you post a comment? Not necessarily. You do not have to comment on every blog you read. However, you should comment as often as possible and make those comments something of value to the blogger.

- You should correct typos and errors in your blogs. This does not mean edit comments you do not really like or do not agree with. This is strictly to correct grammatical or typographical errors.

- Do not write anything you do not want the whole word to know (e.g., details about your spouse, boss, salary, etc.).

Again, there are no hard and fast rules. Go with the rule of respect and common sense, and you cannot go wrong. An open mind can go a long way. For business blogs, make sure your bloggers always stick to your corporate message and communicate professionally and respectfully.

MIND YOUR BLOGGING MANNERS

By Priya Shah

It's about time bloggers set a code of conduct, not only for writing, but also for tolerating what sort of comments they will tolerate on their blogs. A recent New York Times article notes:

"A few high-profile figures in high-tech are proposing a blogger code of conduct to clean up the quality of online discourse. Tim O'Reilly, a conference promoter and book publisher who is credited with coining the term Web 2.0, began working with Jimmy Wales, creator of the communal online encyclopedia Wikipedia, to create a set of guidelines to shape online discussion and debate. Chief among the recommendations is that bloggers consider banning anonymous comments left by visitors to their pages and be able to delete threatening or libelous comments without facing cries of censorship."

Having been at the receiving end of nasty comments myself, I think it's a good start to cleaning up the blogosphere. It's not about restricting freedom of speech. It's about making the blogosphere safer for people who want to express themselves freely without being subjected to cyber-bullying and hate attacks. I believe that my blog is my home online. And it's up to me to decide who I want to allow on my turf.

My personal policy for blogging and commenting is that it should follow the rules of common human decency. I don't mind the comments, just the sentiment behind them. I don't write anything on my blogs that I would not say to someone in real life. Nor would I tolerate comments that I would not tolerate in actual conversation. And that is what blogs are — a conversation.

I do, however, make an exception for critical comments posted with good intention, and reply to these with like intention. Honest criticism is always welcome, because it's what makes blogs so valuable as a medium for marketers to communicate with their audiences.

It's the comments posted solely for the purpose of being nasty that I delete, and I advise you to delete them too. Not because I give a damn for what the "trolls" think, but because I simply choose not to allow negativity into my life.

We believe that feeding the trolls only encourages them. As George Bernard Shaw said, "I learned long ago, never to wrestle with a pig. You get dirty, and besides,

MIND YOUR BLOGGING MANNERS

the pig likes it." Ignoring public attacks is often the best way to contain them.

The Blogger's Code of Conduct guidelines from Tim O'Reilly's pot, are excellent and I agree with them, to a large extent.

1. We take responsibility for our own words and reserve the right to restrict comments on our blog that do not conform to basic civility standards.

2. We won't say anything online that we wouldn't say in person.

3. If tensions escalate, we will connect privately before we respond publicly.

4. When we believe someone is unfairly attacking another, we take action.

5. We do not allow anonymous comments.

6. We ignore the trolls.

7. We encourage blog hosts to enforce more vigorously their terms of service.

Another issue raised by the New York Times article was that of vandalism and misuse of photos posted by well-read bloggers like Heather Armstrong. As a mother, I have (what I believe are) valid concerns for my family's privacy. Because of the likelihood of photographs being copied and vandalized, morphed or misused, I avoid posting any that identify any member of my family clearly, and rarely share anything that's very personal (except my opinions, and some travel photos) on my blogs. E-mail is, and will always be, my preferred medium for sharing personal photos. But that's me.

I think it's the well-read and/or controversial bloggers who are more likely to be targeted by vandals and cyber-bullies (Ah, the price of fame and book deals!). So the ordinary blogger, like you and me, will, hopefully, not have to worry about being targets, except for the occasional troll who wanders along.

The New York Times article also mentions attempts to get bloggers to adhere more strictly to a journalistic code of conduct, which I believe will go a long way in making blogs a more credible source of information and eliminate the objections that some critics have to the "dark side of blogs."

MIND YOUR BLOGGING MANNERS

Bloggers should talk about creating several sets of guidelines for conduct and seals of approval represented by logos. For example, anonymous writing might be acceptable in one set; in another, it would be discouraged. Under a third set of guidelines, bloggers would pledge to get a second source for any gossip or breaking news they write about.

I think anonymous blogging might be valid in countries where political freedom is suppressed, or where certain views might go against religious sentiment. Bloggers wield a great deal of power in the wired world, and increasingly, in the mainstream media. It would be wise for the blogging community to remember that with great power, comes great responsibility, and wield their pens with humility and respect for others.

Now will someone please come up with a solution to zap those spam comment posters?

Priya (pronounced 'pree-yaa') Florence Shah lives in a suburb of India's financial capital, Mumbai. She is an Internet publisher, marketer, entrepreneur, and full-time mom. Priya writes on Internet marketing, search engine optimization, business blogging, RSS technology, personal growth and spirituality, and health and wellness. She helps her clients boost Web traffic, make more profit from their Web sites, and brand themselves online. Priya can be found online at **http://www.priyashah.com/,** **http://www.marketingslave.com/,** *and* **http://www.soulkadee.com/.**

Chapter 5

How to Write a Great Blog

There is an art to blogging and an art to blogging effectively. You do not need any special writing skills to create blogs. You do need some education if you wish to create and write effective blogs. In this chapter I have compiled the best techniques for writing effective blogs.

This list is not complete and is dependent on the type of blog, topic of the blog, target audience, and the attitude of the bloggers who are posting comments on the blog.

How Important Is Your Blog Content?

Your blog content is the most important factor in your blog. The key question is how to determine what good content is. This is not simple to answer, since there are many variables. Primarily, a blog needs to be useful. By useful I mean it has to have content that is meaningful to me. Does it provide the information, conversation, content, and interaction on a topic that I am interested in and is both educational and enlightening?

For businesses, organizations, or causes, you need to define what your target audience is after, design it with content that addresses what your target audience wants, communicate it effectively, and reach out to your readers. Give them what they want, and they will be back. A little research on your target audience can go a long way. Seek out feedback and make changes to your blog accordingly. Your blog readers know what they want, so deliver it to them.

Guidelines for Writing Blogs

- Keeping your blog on topic is critical to prevent you from swaying in directions that will lose your core audience.

- A blog is a compilation of opinions. Encourage others to share opinions, thoughts, and opposing views to keep the blog engaging and interesting. Interject humor and wit when you can.

- Inform your readers. Be factual, accurate, and professional. Ensure your blog is clearly written and without spelling errors.

- Differentiate between fact and opinion. If your post is based on fact, clearly present the fact. If it is your opinion, be sure to make it clear.

- Present timely information. Dated information will clearly indicate your blog is not timely and it will become irrelevant.

- Have consistent blog updates. As your blog grows in readership, your audience will look forward to your scheduled blog posts. Do not disappoint them and do not announce daily updates if you cannot stick to it. Do update your blog as frequently as possible. This not only develops and grows your audience, but also helps you with search engine rankings.

- Be straightforward and simple in your blog entries. Keep them clear, easy to read, and easy to understand.

- Keywords drive search engine rankings. If you want your blog to be visible, you need to insert keywords relevant to your business into your blog posts. Include related keywords in the title and the content post of your blog entries.

- Be patient. You may think your blog is cool and exciting, but it takes time for people to find it and even more time to grow your audience. Despite the claims that once you start a blog zillions of people will flock to it, it is not true. Keep your content relevant and fresh, and your blog audience will grow.

- Links are critical. Link to Web sites, other blogs, books, articles, news, and anything else relevant.

- Keep it brief. Try to get your point across quickly in the fewest number of words. Long posts can lose your readers and get off-topic. However, short blog posts may not contain enough information to be of value. Learn the magic length for your blog and try to stick to it. You may have more success keeping your blog posts shorter and breaking them into multiple posts to capture increased readership through your RSS feeds and search engines.

- Titles attract attention. They should capture the essence of your blog post. Most people scan Web pages and only stop when something catches their attention. If your titles do not attract attention, you will lose potential blog readership. People do not spend long reading blogs; keep it simple and to the point.

- Organize your posts for readability. Keep sentences short and use spacing or bullets to organize thoughts.

- Consistency in approach and tone is important, especially if you win over audiences by with personality.

- Blogging does not require a graduate-level education. Do not over-think it, keep a sense of humor, and do not patronize your readers. You are not writing a term paper. You will not be receiving a grade on it.

- Bold and italics are good for emphasizing key words, phrases, and ideas.

- Jargon and acronyms are bad. Avoid them. You may understand them, but others may not.

- Write in clear, captivating, and descriptive tones. Paint the picture in the reader's mind. Give them the details they crave. Nothing is worse than headlines that capture your interest only to find the blog post has no substance, no descriptive data, and is boring.

- Take a risk. Write outside your comfort zone about topics you have an interest in, want more information about, want to learn about, want to offer your opinion on, etc.

- Be thick-skinned. No matter what you write about and what your opinion is, there are opposing opinions and some all-around hate mongers out there. Your opinions and blog posts may be your opinion or your company position on issues, but there will be opposing thoughts and opinions. Do not take them personally, and do not worry about negativity. It comes with the territory.

You now have a fairly comprehensive list of generalized do's and don'ts, as well as the best practices for writing effective blogs. Next, we will discuss some of the best practices and advice for how to write comments on blogs.

How to Write Comments on Blogs

There are some specific guidelines you can follow when posting comments that will help your reputation as well as your professionalism as a blogger. Write respectfully, intelligently, and support your comments. In the blogosphere, reputation is everything; the few names you see tossed around as "master bloggers" are known mostly by reputation, not because they completed a graduate-level program in blogging.

Your blogs are read by a wide variety of individuals, and some will seek you out for other potential partnerships and for marketing ventures. You never know who will read your blog, so follow the guidelines of professionalism. This is critical for corporate blogging.

It should be clear to other readers of the blogs that you know what you are talking about. In general, it is a good idea to keep your posts short and on point.

Guidelines for Blog Comments

- Keep your comments short and simple.

- Keep your comments relevant, professional, and on topic. Blog administrators will purge offensive material, personal flames, and other inappropriate content. Also, when using someone else's material, give them the appropriate attribution.

- Sign your comments. Include your e-mail address, Web site URL, and blog URL.

- Provide quality comments that add substance and meaning. Fluff or generalized two-word entries are of no value.

- Promote your blog, business, Web site, etc. in your blog posts by either providing a URL and brief description or embedding it into the blog comment so readers can follow your link if they wish.

- If you have nothing useful to add to a blog, do not add anything.

Chapter 6

Building a Blog

L et us get into the process of building our blog. Remember this book is designed to show you how to blog for free, so I will show you several examples of how to build free blogs using the most popular tools on the Internet. Additionally, we will use a commercial blogging application and build a blog to be hosted on a corporate Web site.

If you have your own Web server, domain name or hosting account that supports blog publishing, I recommend you host the blog on your server under your own domain name. While using the hosted solution is perfectly fine with either Blogger or WordPress, it may be difficult to move your blog content to your own server at a later time.

Blogger

Blogger started as a small independent company in the late 1990s. In 2002, Blogger was bought out by Google. Although you go to blogger.com to create your blog, you use your Google account login information to access your blog.

First, go to **www.blogger.com:**

Screenshots © Google Inc. and are reproduced with permission

Click on the "Create Your Blog Now" arrow to continue. If you already have a blog with blogger.com, you simply login to access your account.

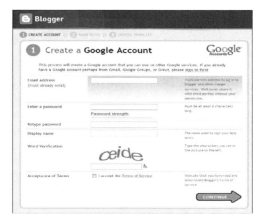

Screenshots © Google Inc. and are reproduced with permission

You must have a Google account to access your blog or create a new blog. Follow the instructions to create a blog or login if you already have an account.

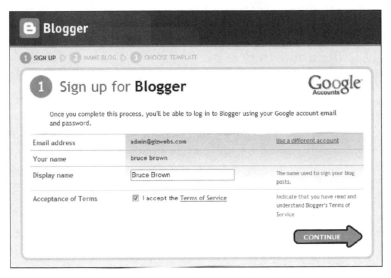

Screenshots © Google Inc. and are reproduced with permission

After you login or create an account, you will see the "Sign up for Blogger" screen. You must specify your display name, which is the name you use to sign your blog posts, and you must check the terms of service.

Screenshots © Google Inc. and are reproduced with permission

Enter the desired title of your blog. In this case, we will create a blog for this book. My blog title is GGWD Blogging for Business (GGWD is the abbreviation for Gizmo Graphics Web Design). I have the option to choose which blog address (URL) I want to use. Note that not all are available (used by other blogs), so click "Check Availability" to ensure it is available. You have the option to host your blog elsewhere (as we have discussed in earlier chapters). Let us try basic setup first, then we will go back and try the advanced setup.

Screenshots © Google Inc. and are reproduced with permission

Choose one of the multiple template formats for your blog. Remember, with Blogger, although it is free, you do lose some control over the look and feel of your blog. Blogger does compensates for this by offering a multitude of great looking templates to choose from. Click the Continue button after you have chosen your template.

Screenshots © Google Inc. and are reproduced with permission

You are done. Your blog is ready for posting.

Screenshots © Google Inc. and are reproduced with permission

Congratulations. You just created your blog. On this screen you can create and publish new blog posts, edit your posts, moderate comments, and compose and save draft blog posts. You can also edit your settings and template design.

On the top right hand side of each page you will see a link to the "Dashboard." This is the central control panel for your blog where you edit all your settings, manage your blog, and read news and features from blogger.com.

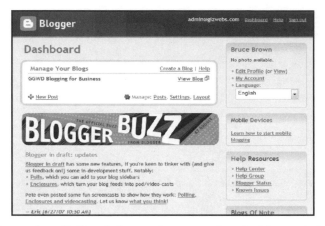

Screenshots © Google Inc. and are reproduced with permission

Let us edit the settings of our blog. Click on the settings link and go through each section to customize your preferences.

Screenshots © Google Inc. and are reproduced with permission

Most of the setting features are self-explanatory and are based on your personal preferences. The BlogSend Address is an e-mail address to send your blog to when it is published, and the Mail-to-Blogger Address is an address you can use to e-mail posts directly to your blog (without having to access your blog).

Screenshots © Google Inc. and are reproduced with permission

The permissions page lets you specify blog authors and assign permission for who can post to your blog and who can read it.

Screenshots © Google Inc. and are reproduced with permission

The template link lets you edit and format your template. Although you have limited control over your template, you do have options.

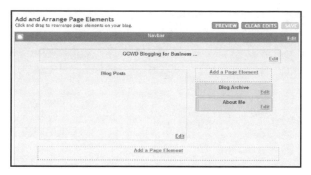

Screenshots © Google Inc. and are reproduced with permission

You can customize quite a few elements and add page elements, images, links, text, and much more. Blogger is configured to add page elements automatically by clicking the "Add a Page Element" link. Page elements are things such as Google Adsense accounts, labels, pictures, and text, as well as a profile of yourself, which can essentially be plugged into your blog quickly and easily.

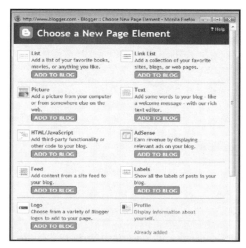

Screenshots © Google Inc. and are reproduced with permission

You can also change your template quickly and easily with the click of a button.

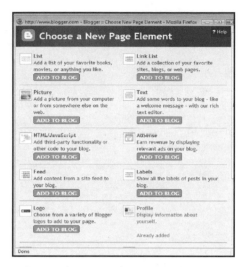

Screenshots © Google Inc. and are reproduced with permission

We have completed our blog, customized it, and are ready to publish our first post.

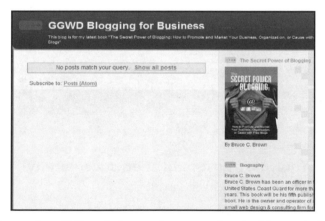

Screenshots © Google Inc. and are reproduced with permission

Navigate back to the "Posting" tab of your Blogger site to create your first blog post. Simply type in the title and post contents, and you are ready to publish.

Screenshots © Google Inc. and are reproduced with permission

Click the "Publish Post" button to publish your new post. Note that your draft post will be automatically saved if you wish to save it for editing or posting at a later time. Once you publish your data, you will receive a confirmation from Blogger.

Screenshots © Google Inc. and are reproduced with permission

You may now view your blog. Since Blogger automates the ping process for you, the notification service is kicked off each time a blog post occurs.

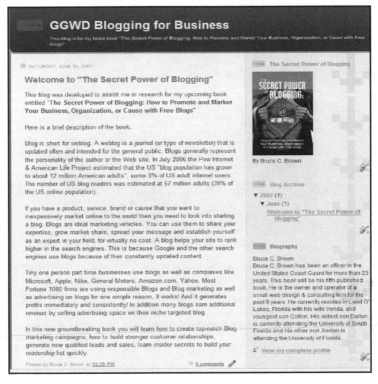

Screenshots © Google Inc. and are reproduced with permission

Since we enabled e-mail notification of each post in the "Settings" section, you will receive an e-mail after each blog post is published.

You can also e-mail blog posts to Blogger. Blogger provides you with the e-mail address; simply create the e-mail and send it and your post will automatically be published to your blog.

At this point, you have created a blog, published several posts, and have customized the look and feel. Blogger is completely free, easy to use, and does not place any advertising on it. You have dozens of templates to choose from and, although you do not have total control over your blog, it is a great way to get started.

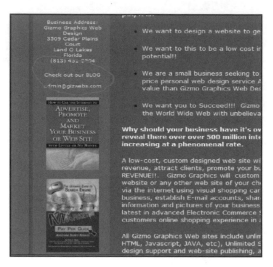

Screenshots © Google Inc. and are reproduced with permission

Blogger does support syndication feeds for your Web site. Syndication means that when you publish your blog, Blogger automatically generates a machine-readable representation of your blog that can be picked up and displayed on other Web sites and information aggregation tools. The setup within Blogger is very simple.

Blogger supports Atom, which is a syndication format or feed for your blog. When a regularly updated site has a feed, people can subscribe to it using software for reading syndicated content called a "newsreader." People like using readers for blogs because it allows them to catch up on all their favorites at once and avoid navigating multiple Web sites.

When you activate Atom syndication, Blogger automatically generates a machine-readable version of your blog that can be picked up and displayed in a variety of ways on newsreaders, Web sites, and handheld devices. There are already a bunch of newsreaders that support Atom, including NewzCrawler, NewsGator, NetNewsWire, Shrook, RSSOwl, and BottomFeeder.

In the settings control panel, you will want to turn on some features. You can turn on verification functions that require individuals posting to your blog to authenticate. This is a critical step to prevent spam posts from hitting your blog.

Screenshots © Google Inc. and are reproduced with permission

Help is readily available in Blogger by clicking the "Help" link in the upper right hand corner of any page.

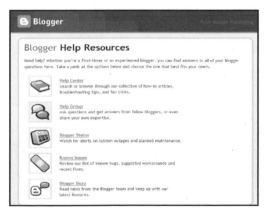

Screenshots © Google Inc. and are reproduced with permission

Hosting a Blogger.com Blog on Your Own Web Server

Let us take a look at how to configure Blogger using the advanced setup to host the blog on your own Web servers or hosted Web account.

With an existing blog at Blogger.com, you may switch, at any time, from the hosted blogging Web site to your own Web site by clicking on the "Publishing" link and then switching to custom domain link.

Screenshots © Google Inc. and are reproduced with permission

Simply enter the URL for your blog and blog readers will be redirected to your hosted URL. The missing files host allows Blogger to look back at your original blog URL in the event it cannot find files at your hosted site.

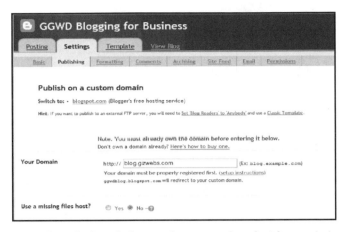

Screenshots © Google Inc. and are reproduced with permission

Let us set up a blog from scratch and host it on our own Web site. First, go to **www.blogger.com:**

Screenshots © Google Inc. and are reproduced with permission

Click on the "Create Your Blog Now" arrow to continue. If you already have a blog with **blogger.com**, you simply login to access your account.

Screenshots © Google Inc. and are reproduced with permission

Follow the instructions to create a blog or login if you already have an account.

Screenshots © Google Inc. and are reproduced with permission

Click the "Advanced Blog Setup" link to access the advanced setup screen. You will enter your blog title, listing options, and detailed server information. You will need to enter your FTP server information, blog filename, and FTP access information.

Screenshots © Google Inc. and are reproduced with permission

Once this is completed, you are ready to customize any other settings and publish your blog.

Screenshots © Google Inc. and are reproduced with permission

You will be given a confirmation if your FTP publishing update is successful, and you can click the "View Blog" link to view your blog. All the other features are available, giving you control over the template, style, and settings, and you can even publish posts via e-mail to your own Qeb server. The best part is you really do not even need to have a new Web site or domain name for your blog — you can host it right alongside your main Web site.

Screenshots © Google Inc. and are reproduced with permission

In the following image, you will see that our sample blog was created via the FTP publishing feature and is hosted on our main domain URL. For businesses or organizations that wish to maintain the utmost professional Web site, it is best to host the blog on your own URL instead of a free hosting service. Additionally, since you own the domain name and Web server/hosting, you have ultimate control over the data. Keep in mind that you may have multiple blogs with Blogger; some may be hosted on Blogger, and some may be hosted yourself, but all are managed from the main control panel.

Screenshots © Google Inc. and are reproduced with permission

WordPress

WordPress is immensely popular in the blogging community. It is by far the most powerful and customizable application with many available plug-ins. WordPress is simple to set up and takes about five minutes from start to finish. We will use WordPress to set up a blog for Atlantic Publishing Company who would like to use a blog to promote its new book releases and other news and information.

Establishing a WordPress Account

First, go to **wordpress.com** and click on "Start your Free WordPress Blog" link.

Screenshots © WordPress and are reproduced with permission

You need to establish a username, enter your e-mail address, comply with terms and conditions, then click the "Next" button.

Screenshots © WordPress and are reproduced with permission

WordPress will use your username as part of your domain name — in this case, **atlanticpub.worldpress.com**. Enter your blog title, language, and click the "Privacy" box to allow your blog to be publicized to search engines, such as Google and Technorati. You will be given the confirmation screen, which tells you that an e-mail has been sent to you to confirm your account.

Once you confirm your login through the e-mail activation process, you may use the provided password and your username to log into the blog site. Your basic initial blog is now completed and published.

Screenshots © WordPress and are reproduced with permission

Additionally, you will receive a confirmation e-mail that contains all your critical account information, along with helpful links, frequently asked questions, and other information to access, update, and publish your blog.

I recommend you start by clicking on the "My Account" link and the "Edit Profile" option to start customization. Update the basic information such as name, profile, and your password.

Although it took only a few minutes to actually create the blog, it is certainly does not have the look and feel we desire at this time.

Customizing Your WordPress Blog

I recommend you start by clicking on the "Options" link in your WordPress account to begin customizing your blog. The options link allows you to update your general settings, as well as customize most other publishing options.

Screenshots © WordPress and are reproduced with permission

Under the "Privacy" link, selected options for your blog to appear in search engines and public listings in Wordpress.com to ensure maximum visibility.

Click on the "Presentation" tab to begin the process of selecting a site template and adding widgets and extras to your blog.

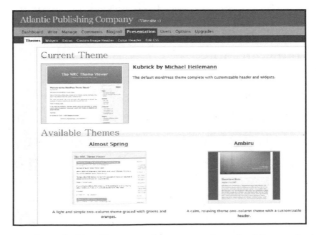

Screenshots © WordPress and are reproduced with permission

Go through each tab (themes, widgets, extras, image header, etc.) to customize your blog to your desired settings. You have great flexibility in choosing the final appearance of your blog. Simply drag and drop your desired widgets into the sidebar of your blog. For widgets that require customization, click on the blue customization tab within the widget on your sidebar to customize the settings and preferences.

Screenshots © WordPress and are reproduced with permission

The "Write" link is where you will post blogs. We will discuss that more later. The "Manage" link lets you manage your blogs, uploads, imports, exports, and delete individual posts. The "Comments" tab allows you to search, view, edit, and delete comments from your blog.

We mentioned the blogroll previously. This is where you can add your favorite or relevant blogs that have content your audience may be interested in. Maintaining your blogroll is a great way to grow your audience. As you can see below, this process is very simple.

Screenshots © WordPress and are reproduced with permission

You can also create and specify categories for each blogroll listing. If you need to change anything later, just click the edit link to change any of your information, links, or category selections.

The "Write" feature is what you will use to publish blog posts. You will find more robust features than Blogger. You can use pre-edited HTML formatted text or format on the fly in the entry form. You can attach images, upload files, slideshows, videos (note: your free account has a 50MB capacity limit), and trackbacks.

The "Dashboard" is the main control panel for your blog. You can publish posts, view comments, edit your site, change preferences, and edit your template, layout, widgets, and extras.

Screenshots © WordPress and are reproduced with permission

I highly recommend you spend some time on the discussion forums, help files, and other readily available resources for WordPress. There is a wealth of information available, as well as an abundance of widgets you can use to customize and enhance your blog. At this point, the blog has been published. All we need to do is link it up with our Web site and start promoting it.

Office 2007 and Blog Posts

If you use Office 2007, you will find that Word now has built-in support for blogging. To use this feature, simply open Word 2007, click on New, then Blog Post. You will be given a drop down menu of options to configure the first time you use this feature. As you can see, Word supports Blogger, Windows Live, Sharepoint Blog, TypePad, WordPress, and others. You will need to set up your account information, username/password, etc., and then you can simply publish to your blog directly from Word.

Other Free Blogging Applications

I have mentioned other excellent, free blogging applications throughout this book, and here is a more thorough list. A fairly comprehensive listing is available at **http://asymptomatic.net/ blogbreakdown.htm**.

- Movable Type (**http://www.movabletype.org/**)

- Live Journal (**http://www.livejournal.com/**)

- ClearBlogs (**http://clearblogs.com/**)

- Soul Cast (**http://www.soulcast.com/**)

- Blog.com (**http://blog.com/**)

- TeamPage5 (**http://www.tractionsoftware.com**)

For more information, visit their Web sites.

Commercial Blogging Applications

There is no shortage of commercial blogging applications. I have found that WordPress is extremely powerful, and it, as well as Blogger, are great choices for those on a budget. However, if you want more functionality and control over the design and appearance of your blog, there are many commercial applications you can purchase. These include:

- TypePad (**www.typepad.com**)

- Miniweb 2.0 Blog Writer (**http://www.miniweb2.com**)

- ExpressionEngine (**http://expressionengine.com/**)

We have reviewed many blog applications and set up two fully functional, completely free blogs. There are many more open source, freeware, shareware, and other versions of blog software available on the Web. Let us move on and take a look at the relationship between your Web site and your blog.

A Final Note

You will find that your audience wants to know who you are. Include an author biography on your blog pages. It sounds silly, but you can build a strong bond and lasting relationship once your readers know and trust you, your opinions, and your advice.

Chapter 7

The Relationship Between Your Blog & Your Web Site

Your Web site and your blog share a unique relationship with each other. You need to leverage each to its fullest potential while driving visitors to both. You want to capture your blog audience and drive them to your site to purchase your products and/or services, donate to your cause, or join your organization. Equally important, you want to drive Web site visitors to your blog since that is your primary means of communication with your audience.

Your blog needs to complement your Web site, and your Web site needs to complement your blog. Exactly what does that mean? If you have a Web-based company that sells a specific product, car stereo equipment for example, then it would be expected that your Web site would have a variety of products, information, prices, reviews, and the capability to place an order. Depending on the intent or purpose of your blog, you may want it to promote specials, publish your personal reviews and opinions of audio gear, and publish information to the general public on what gear is best for what vehicle, etc. You may even want to use your blog as an expert advice page where audience members ask you for advice about which products you recommend for their automobiles, and then you can hopefully refer them to your Web site for the sale. The key is that your blog needs to be relevant to your company mission, purpose, products, or marketing plans. Having a company dedicated to audio equipment with a blog on the best surfing spots on the outer banks of North Carolina might be cool, but that blog is not really going to generate the profit return you might want it to. Likewise, your Web site represents your company. You must clearly identify your blog on your home page. Since Web pages are mostly static, the blog is your tool to show off your personality, interact with customers, and win them over.

Blogs are very attractive to search engines. In the next chapter, I will talk more about blogging and Web site traffic, but for now, understand that blogs get indexed by search engines and, in fact, may get indexed sooner than Web pages. There are many places you can search blogs, such as **http://blogsearch.google. com/**, **http://technorati.com/**, **http://www.blogsearchengine. com/**, **http://www.blog-search.com/**, **http://www.icerocket.com/**, **http://www.ysearchblog.com/** (Yahoo® blogs only), **http://blogs. gigablast.com/**, and **http://www.ask.com/?tool=bls**.

Remember, you can have multiple blogs on a variety of topics. Do not limit yourself. You can have as many blogs as you want, link all of them back to your Web site, and have your Web site link to them.

Linking to Your Blog from Your Site

Linking your Web site to your blog is as simple as linking to any other Web page or site. Using your Web site editor open your home page and insert a prominent link to your blog site. In the examples below, we have placed links to our blog sites:

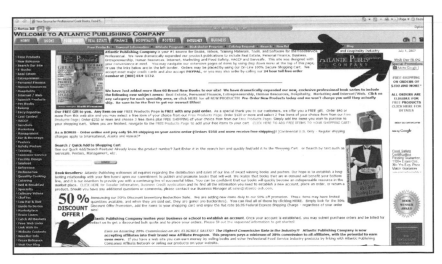

How Your Blog Helps Your Web Site

There is a direct relationship between you blog and your Web site, and that is in search engine visibility. Search engines thrive on blog posts because the content is updated often, and this indexing of your blog will result in improved search engine rankings for your blog and your Web site. Since you can target very specific interests with your blog, you can have multiple blogs each targeting a specific niche area, all drawing visitors back to your main Web site. Remember to load your blogs with appropriate keywords to increase visibility in search engines.

Use the features in your blogging application to segment your posts by category. This allows your audience to find specific posts of interest to their topic of interest. Remember, the most powerful feature of the blog is the amount of times your blog will be linked to, shared, and republished throughout the Web.

Your blog complements your Web site by allowing you to add fresh content often and drawing in potential Web site visitors. Your blog pumps fresh content to your customers and allows those same customers the ability to post comments and interact with you.

Your Blog Domain

As you know, there are many options for hosting your blog and the domain name you will choose for your blog. While using the default blogspot.com or wordpress.com address is acceptable, you are much better off using your own domain names. Additionally, you will have better search results using your own domain name in search engine rankings. In other words, you will attain better search engine visibility by using **http://www.gizwebs.com/blog.htm** rather than **http://blog. gizwebs.com,** which is a mapped domain. This is certainly not the final word on this subject, and you will find varying opinions on it. The nice thing with Blogger is that you can use the Blogger interface, publish via FTP to your own server (and refresh data with the click of a button), and use your domain name hosting account, such as **http://www.gizwebs.com/blog. htm**. When possible, if you are hosting your blog on your Web site, you should match the design, look, and feel of your blog to your Web site. Place links between your blog and your Web site and post them often. The more, the better.

Chapter 8

Blogging and Web Site Traffic

One of the main purposes of your blog, aside from marketing and communications, is to increase visibility in search engines and draw more potential customers and visitors to your Web site. Effectively designed Web sites and blogs can significantly increase your visibility in search engine rankings.

Optimizing Your Blog

If you have read any of my previous books, you know that search engine optimization and increasing Web site traffic is a slow path to follow. There is no magic formula, no one can "guarantee" you top rankings, and no matter what you read, it takes time, patience, and diligence — it cannot be done overnight. Blogging does not change that; in fact, you will not see significant results for up to three months after you have begun the optimization process. That said, your blog is an effective tool to increase site traffic.

It is easier to get top ranking with your blog than it is with your Web site. Why? Simply because an search-engine optimized (SEO) blog, which is updated frequently, tends to get indexed and spidered by the search engines more often than static HTML Web sites. Since you link your blogs back to your Web site, as your blogs grow in popularity and search engine rankings, so does the resulting traffic to your Web site.

Tags

The use of tags will help you organize your blog posts, and by categorizing them, help others find your posts by "tag" or category. Specific advice on Technorati tags can be found at **http://support.technorati.com/support/siteguide/tags** and the listing of the current, most popular tags is available at **http://technorati.com/tag/**. Both WordPress and Blogware support categories and RSS/Atom Feeds (as do most other major blogware programs). Simply choose a category (you create your own categories when you publish your posts), and those categories will be read as "tags."

If you are using blog software that does not support the use of categories, you can use a Technorati tag by including a special link in the body of your blog post, such as: <a ref="http://technorati.com/tag/[tagname]" rel="tag">[tagname]</a>. You can tag anything you want, but it should be descriptive enough to identify the blog post and must be relevant to the content of the post. Be sure to include the rel="tag" in your tag code. Make sure "ping" is set to automatic to post your Technorati tags.

Ideally, you will create a tag for each keyword in every post. This is a laborious process. If you are using Blogger, you have to use the manual method; however, if you are using WordPress, there is a plugin called "SimpleTags," which automates the process. You can download it at **http://www.broobles.com/scripts/simpletags**. Tagging works, and it will draw more traffic to your blogs.

Review both your blog posts and your Web site content for keyword-rich phrases. Remove extraneous material that adds little or no value and replace with proper, spoken English phrases loaded with key words and key phrases. Be diverse in your phraseology. By this I mean use multiple descriptions for similar items because others may search using a variety of phrases, such as "Web design, "Website design," "Web site design," etc.

Trackbacks

Effective use of trackbacks in your blog posts will dramatically increase visibility and traffic for your blog. Trackbacks are more than just placing a URL link in your blog to another Web site or blog. That is a great idea, but trackbacks take it a step further.

Here is an example: I have just read a blog that has some great information. I would like to place a link to that blog on my blog. So, I click on "permalink" on the other blog and paste it into my blog post. Since I want to let the author/owner of the other blog know that I have published a post that talks about his blog, I am going to go back to his blog and click on the "Trackback URL." I need to copy this URL (note this is not the same URL to the blog), and I am going to paste this Trackback URL into my blog post in the "Trackback" link box. When I publish my blog post, my blog tells the other blog that it is has linked to it. On the other blog, you will see a link under the trackback links to my blog, so they know I linked to them and provided a link back to my blog. It sounds confusing, but is easy and effective.

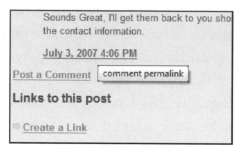

The number one rule is that if you find a site or blog you like, bookmark and visit often. Comment on the blog posts when they are of interest or you have an opinion to share. Subscribe to the blog's RSS/Atom feeds. Share articles among blogs and use trackbacks to other articles of relevance. You will find the community that writes articles and advice is a great source for growing Web site traffic.

Links

Request links from similar or relevant blogs and link to them in return. Write quality, relevant articles and publish them at other article Web sites with a link back to your site and blog. This is a huge way to increase traffic.

Linking from your site or blog to others is a must. Do not sign up with a junk link service which links you with 10,000 useless sites; you will drop out of the search engines fast. Link with quality blogs or sites that have complimentary or relevant content.

Use your blogroll. A blogroll is simply a collection of blogs that you visit often, or feel are useful, and you choose to list them on your blog. This is a great way to build relationships with other bloggers. Keep your blogroll a living list; add to it often and as appropriate.

Blog Directories

Do a quick search on "blog directories" and you will find dozens of directories you can submit your blog URL to. There is nothing wrong with this technique. Although it will take some time, you will see results. Here are two: **http://www.icerocket.com** and **http://www.bloggernity.com**.

Tips for Web Site Optimization

If you want to get the best results from search engines, here are some tips that you should follow to optimize your Web site:

- Make sure that you have at least 200 words of content on each page. Although you may have some Web pages on which it may be difficult to put even close to 200 words, come as close as you can since search engines will give better results to pages with more content.

- Make sure the content contains those important keywords and key phrases that you have researched and are the most common phrases potential customers might use to search for your products or services. It is important to use your keywords heavily on your Web pages. Use key phrases numerous times, placing them close to the top of the page. Place key phrases between head tags in the first two paragraphs of your page. Place key phrases in bold type at least once on each page.

- No matter how much content you have after incorporating keywords and key phrases, make sure that the content you have is still understandable and readable in plain language. A common mistake is to stack a Web site full of so many keywords and key phrases that the page is no longer understandable or readable to the Web site visitor — a sure bet to lose potential customers quickly.

- The keywords and key phrases you use in the content of your Web site should also be included in the tags of your Web site, such as meta tags, ALT tags, head tags, and title tags.

- Add extra pages to your Web site, even if they may not at first seem directly relevant. The more Web pages you have, the more pages search engines find and link to. Extra pages can include tips, tutorials, product information, resource information, and any other information or data that is pertinent to the product or service you are selling.

- Design pages so they are easily navigated by search engine spiders and Web crawlers. Search engines prefer text over graphics and also prefer HTML over other page formats.

- Do not use frames. Search engines have difficulty following them and so will your site visitors. The best advice we can give on frames is to never use them.

- Limit the use of Macromedia Flash and other design applications, as most search engines have trouble reading them, hurting you in search engine listings.

- Consider creating a site map of all pages within your Web site. While not necessarily the most useful tool to site visitors, it does greatly improve the search engine's capacity to property index all your Web site pages.

- Many Web sites use a left-hand navigational bar. However, the algorithm that many spiders and Web crawlers use will have this read before the main content of your Web site. Make sure you use keywords within the navigation and, if using images for your navigational buttons, ensure you use the ALT tags loaded with appropriate keywords.

- Ensure that all pages have links back to the home page.

- Use copyright and about us pages.

- Try using a text browser, such as Lynx, to examine your site. Features such as JavaScript, cookies, session IDs, frames, DHTML, or Flash keep search engine spiders from properly crawling your entire Web site.

- Implement the use of the robots.txt file on your Web server. This file tells crawlers which directories can or cannot be crawled. You can find out more information on the robots.txt file by visiting **http://www.robotstxt.org/wc/ faq.html.**

- Avoid tricks intended to improve search engine rankings. A good rule of thumb is whether you would feel comfortable explaining what you have done to a Web site that competes with you. Another useful test is to ask, "Does this help my users? Would I do this if search engines didn't exist?"

- Do not participate in link schemes designed to increase your site's ranking. Do not link to Web spammers, as your own ranking will be negatively affected by those links.

- Consider implementing cascading style sheets into your Web site to control site layout and design. Search engines prefer CSS-based sites and typically score them higher in the search rankings.

Chapter 9

Promoting Your Blog

In this chapter we will discuss some techniques you can use to promote your blog, beyond simply optimizing the content for the search engines. You may find some of these techniques very obvious or very minor; however, in an overall marketing and promotion campaign, they are all very effective and can dramatically increase the visibility of your blog.

- Place your Web site links on your blog and vice versa.

- Place your Web site URL and blog URL on your business cards, stationery, letterhead, and corporate memos.

- Place your site URL and blog URL in your e-mail signature.

- Use promotional materials (bumper stickers, key chains, pencils, T-shirts, etc) with your blog's URL.

- Include your Web site URL and blog URL in all print advertising (newsletters, flyers, ads, articles, etc.).

- Distribute press releases for news, information, or product releases and include your Web site URL and blog URL.

- Write articles and submit them to professional e-zines, article directories, and others to publish. Be sure to include a release allowing your article to be reprinted or redistributed, but only with proper attribution to you (at minimum include your name, company, Web site URL and blog URL).

- Even though you have ping turned on for your blogs, use a free pinging service to hit all the major search engines. It is quick and very simple. I recommend **http://pingomatic. com**, **http://feedshark.brainbliss.com**, and **http:// technorati.com/ping**.

- Submit your blog and RSS feed to directory services. A good list is available online at **http://www.toprankblog. com/rss-blog-directories/**.

- Implement an AdSense program in your Web site and blogs. For more details on AdSense, visit **http://www. google.com/adsense**, or pick up a copy of my book *The Ultimate Guide to Search Engine Marketing – Pay Per Click Advertising Secrets Revealed*.

- If you are using Blogger, ensure you allow your blog to be added to the Blogger listing. Details about this are at **http://help.blogger.com/bin/answer.py?answer=41373**.

- Actively comment on others' blogs; they will actively comment on yours.

- Sign up for a free Feedburner account (**http://www. feedburner.com**) and use it to promote your blog.

- Offer to exchange links with other Web sites and blogs.

- Start a contest that requires people to visit your blog. Sure, you are forcing their hand, but people like to win stuff, or even try to win stuff, so take advantage of the free traffic.

- Post quality content on a regular, consistent basis.

- Use meta description and keywords in your blog pages.

- Tag your content with **http://digg.com/**, **http://del.icio.us/**, and others.

- Join online discussion groups and forums, establish yourself as an expert in your market, and always leave your blog URL with your forum posts.

- Interact with other bloggers at **http://www.mybloglog.com/**. This gives you great stats and indexes your blog within their community listings.

- Use podcasts to promote your Web site, company, or blog.

The best advice of all is to simply have patience. As with everything, there is no magic solution to promote your blog. It is done over time, one blog post at a time. Use the solutions and recommendations provided where possible, and over time, you will see the results. It takes time, often months, to build visibility in search engines, and see the increased traffic.

Chapter 10

The Legalities of Blogging

I n this chapter, I want to bring your attention to some important resources and laws that affect blogging. First and foremost, one of the best sources of information about legal matters on the Internet is the nonprofit Electronic Frontier Foundation. EFF has a wealth of information on its Web site, located at **http://www.eff.org.** Here are a few areas of the law you need to know about.

Communications Decency Act

Congress passed the Communications Decency Act specifically to:

- promote the continued development of the Internet and other interactive computer services and other interactive media;

- preserve the vibrant and competitive free market that presently exists for the Internet and other interactive computer services, unfettered by Federal or State regulation;

- encourage the development of technologies which maximize user control over what information is received by individuals, families, and schools who use the Internet and other interactive computer services;

- remove disincentives for the development and utilization of blocking and filtering technologies that empower parents to restrict their children's access to objectionable or inappropriate online material; and

- ensure vigorous enforcement of Federal criminal laws to deter and punish trafficking in obscenity, stalking, and harassment by means of computer;

Section 230 of the Communications Security Act was enacted to ensure that providers and users of "interactive computer services" would not be exposed to liability as "publishers" of any information provided by another "information content provider." In other words, Section 230 was designed to afford some protection to bloggers.

This section provides limited immunity by stating that "no provider or user of an interactive computer service shall be treated as the publisher or speaker of any information provided by another information content provider." The Act further defines "interactive computer service" (ICS) as "any information service, system, or access software provider that provides or enables computer access by multiple users to a computer server, including specifically a service or system that provides access to the Internet and such systems operated or services offered by libraries or educational institutions."

Information content provider (ICP) is defined as "any person or entity that is responsible, in whole or in part, for the creation or development of information provided through the Internet or any other" ICS. We will discuss this law in greater detail, but it is important that you know and understand exactly what this law provides and what it does not provide in the form of protection and immunity from prosecution.

The Communications Decency Act U.S. Code Title 47 Section 230

§ 230. Protection for private blocking and screening of offensive material

(a) Findings

The Congress finds the following:

(1) The rapidly developing array of Internet and other interactive computer services available to individual Americans represent an extraordinary advance in the availability of educational and informational resources to our citizens.

(2) These services offer users a great degree of control over the information that they receive, as well as the potential for even greater control in the future as technology develops.

(3) The Internet and other interactive computer services offer a forum for a true diversity of political discourse, unique opportunities for cultural development, and myriad avenues for intellectual activity.

(4) The Internet and other interactive computer services have flourished, to the benefit of all Americans, with a minimum of government regulation.

(5) Increasingly Americans are relying on interactive media for a variety of political, educational, cultural, and entertainment services.

(b) Policy

It is the policy of the United States —

(1) to promote the continued development of the Internet and other interactive computer services and other interactive media;

(2) to preserve the vibrant and competitive free market that presently exists for the Internet and other interactive computer services, unfettered by Federal or State regulation;

(3) to encourage the development of technologies which maximize user control over what information is received by individuals, families, and schools who use the Internet and other interactive computer services;

(4) to remove disincentives for the development and utilization of blocking and filtering technologies that empower parents to restrict their children's access to objectionable or inappropriate online material; and

(5) to ensure vigorous enforcement of Federal criminal laws to deter and punish trafficking in obscenity, stalking, and harassment by means of computer.

(c) Protection for "Good Samaritan" blocking and screening of offensive material

(1) Treatment of publisher or speaker

No provider or user of an interactive computer service shall be treated as the publisher or speaker of any information provided by another information content provider.

(2) Civil liability

No provider or user of an interactive computer service shall be held liable on account of —

(A) any action voluntarily taken in good faith to restrict access to or availability of material that the provider or user considers to be obscene, lewd, lascivious, filthy, excessively violent, harassing, or otherwise objectionable, whether or not such material is constitutionally protected; or

(B) any action taken to enable or make available to information content providers or others the technical means to restrict access to material described in paragraph (1).

(d) Obligations of interactive computer service

A provider of interactive computer service shall, at the time of entering an agreement with a customer for the provision of interactive computer service and in a manner deemed appropriate by the provider, notify such customer that parental control protections (such as computer hardware, software, or filtering services) are commercially available that may assist the customer in limiting access to material that is harmful to minors. Such notice shall identify, or provide the customer with access to information identifying, current providers of such protections.

(e) Effect on other laws

(1) No effect on criminal law

Nothing in this section shall be construed to impair the

enforcement of section 223 or 231of this title, chapter 71 (relating to obscenity) or 110 (relating to sexual exploitation of children) of title 18, or any other Federal criminal statute.

(2) No effect on intellectual property law

Nothing in this section shall be construed to limit or expand any law pertaining to intellectual property.

(3) State law

Nothing in this section shall be construed to prevent any State from enforcing any State law that is consistent with this section. No cause of action may be brought and no liability may be imposed under any State or local law that is inconsistent with this section.

(4) No effect on communications privacy law

Nothing in this section shall be construed to limit the application of the Electronic Communications Privacy Act of 1986 or any of the amendments made by such Act, or any similar State law.

(f) Definitions

As used in this section:

(1) Internet

The term "Internet" means the international computer network of both Federal and non-Federal interoperable packet switched data networks.

(2) Interactive computer service

The term "interactive computer service" means any information service, system, or access software provider that provides or enables computer access by multiple users to a computer server, including specifically a service or system that provides access to the Internet and such systems operated or services offered by libraries or educational institutions.

(3) Information content provider

The term "information content provider" means any person or entity that is responsible, in whole or in part, for the creation or development of information provided through the Internet or any other interactive computer service.

(4) Access software provider

The term "access software provider" means a provider of software (including client or server software), or enabling tools that do any one or more of the following:

(A) filter, screen, allow, or disallow content;

(B) pick, choose, analyze, or digest content; or

(C) transmit, receive, display, forward, cache, search, subset, organize, reorganize, or translate content.

Can Bloggers Publish Whatever They Want?

Absolutely, positively no! The best advice is to keep your blogs factual, professional, courteous, and relevant. There is no reason a blog for a corporation, organization, or worthy cause should be involved in slanderous or libelous blog postings in the first place. There have been recent court cases in which bloggers have lost large settlements for what they have posted online, including an $11.3 million lawsuit in Florida. This appears to be a growing trend, as various bloggers are being taken to court for what they have posted.

How Am I Protected as a Blogger?

As a blogger, it is important that you understand and recognize the fact that you may be held responsible for what you say. Section 230 of the Communications Decency Act provides you with protection for "user-generated" content that may be published on your blog (there are some exceptions that we will discuss).

So if Section 230 affords you protection, why are people paying millions of dollars in libel and slander lawsuits? The reason is that you are responsible for what you post as a blogger; however, the law, which was designed to promote free speech, protects you (as an ISP, Webmaster, administrator, etc.) from the content that "other" bloggers may post on your blog. But it does not provide any protection for federal crimes or intellectual property violations. This means that you can be held liable if any of these types of activities take place on your Web site or blog.

How Do I Avoid Legal Problems?

Keep in mind that the law surrounding the Internet and online communications is changing all the time and, as more blog-related cases make it through United States courts, these decisions may ultimately affect the law or the interpretation of the law. Keep vigilant of the ever-changing landscape of legal issues related to blogging.

- Include a disclaimer on your blog related to privacy and monitor for criminal behavior and intellectual rights infringements. Keep your blog on topic, and this should never be an issue. Clearly indicate you will release privacy information (usernames, real names, e-mail addresses, contact or personal information) to law enforcement authorities pursuant to a criminal investigation.

- Do not allow copyrighted material to be published on your blog. Do not allow criminal conduct, comments, or discussions on your blogs. Remove this type of content immediately.

SPAM Law

I have covered the subject of spam in great detail in my book *The Complete Guide to E-mail Marketing: How to Create Successful, Spam-free Campaigns to Reach Your Target Audience and Increase Sales.* The CAN-SPAM Act of 2003 applies to you if you are going to harvest or collect e-mails from your blogs and use them in e-zines or e-mail campaigns. You must include specific information, including opt-out instructions and your physical mailing address. You can read all the rules and requirements on the Federal Trade Commission Web site at **http://www.ftc.gov/bcp/conline/pubs/ buspubs/canspam.shtm**. In your e-mail blasts you may not use false or misleading information in the header or subject lines, you must identify yourself, and you absolutely include a working opt-out solution.

Journalism Shield Laws

Are bloggers journalists and are they protected from revealing sources just as similar laws protect journalists? Even though bloggers are often journalists by profession, the laws protecting bloggers as journalists is a very gray area. A "shield law" provides a news reporter or journalist with the right to refuse to testify about information and/or sources of information obtained during the course of gathering or disseminating news information. Currently, there is no federal shield law, and the rules vary from state to state. The shield law is designed to protect journalists, thus the debate about whether bloggers are journalists. A blogger must be able to substantiate that they meet the definition of a journalist, which has proven to be very difficult without education, training, and credentials. The bottom line is if you do not work for a newsgathering organization or company, you are probably not protected. But there is hope with the Free Flow of Information Act, which may afford the same protection to bloggers as it does journalists.

The following article, taken from **http://dodd.senate.gov/index. php?q=node/3862**, demonstrates that the government is working toward the free flow of information:

> U.S. Sens. Dick Lugar (R-IN) and Chris Dodd (D-CT) today [May 2, 2007] introduced the Free Flow of Information Act, which seeks to protect the public's right to information through a free press. Senators Graham, Domenici, and Landrieu joined as original cosponsors of this resolution. This legislation provides journalists with certain rights and abilities to seek sources and report appropriate information without fear of intimidation or imprisonment. U.S. Reps. Rick Boucher (D-VA) and Mike Pence (R-IN) introduced companion legislation in the House of Representatives.

> This   legislation   confirms   America's   Constitutional

commitment to press freedom and advances our foreign policy initiatives to promote and protect democracy," Lugar said. "We must lead by example and the role of the media as a conduit between government and the citizens it serves cannot be devalued."

"We enter dangerous territory for a democracy when journalists are hauled into court and threatened with imprisonment if they don't divulge their sources," said Dodd. "Forty nine states and the District of Columbia have already recognized the need for a reporter shield by enacting protection on the state level either through legislation or court decisions. The Free Flow of Information Act that Senator Lugar and I are introducing today simply extends that widely-recognized protection to the federal courts. This legislation should not be viewed as a privilege for reporters, but as a protection of every American citizen's right to information and their ability to inform themselves. It is an important first step toward rebalancing the pursuit of justice and the distribution of truth."

The bill would set national standards that must be met before a federal entity may issue a subpoena to a member of the news media in any federal criminal or civil case. It would set out certain tests that civil litigants or prosecutors must meet before they can force a journalist to turn over information. For example, litigants or prosecutors must show that they have tried unsuccessfully to get the information in other ways and that the information is essential to the case. These standards were based on Justice Department guidelines and common law standards.

Additional protections are included to ensure that

information will be disclosed in cases where the information is critical to prevent death or bodily harm or in cases that relate to the unlawful disclosure of trade secrets. The bill would permit a reporter to be compelled to reveal source information when disclosure is necessary to prevent imminent and actual harm to national security. Finally, the bill would provide protections to ensure that source information can be provided when personal health records and financial records were disclosed in violation of federal law.

By providing the courts with a framework for compelled disclosure, the legislation would promote greater transparency of government, maintain the ability of the courts to operate effectively and protect whistleblowers who identify government or corporate misdeeds.

Privacy

You cannot have full control over the posting of information on your blog at all times. Likewise, you can only take so much action to prevent criminal activities or those involving slanderous or libelous blog postings by others. You must include a disclaimer on your blog and Web site related to privacy and monitoring for criminal behavior and intellectual rights infringements. Keep your blog on topic, and this should never been an issue for you. An example of a robust privacy policy is at **http://www.bigfatblog. com/about/privacy/**.

Deleting Content from Your Blog

This one will drive you crazy. You own your Web site and your blog. However, you do not necessarily own the content of your blog. If you allow others to post comments and add content or reviews, you do not own this content. This is considered an original work and is protected under copyright laws as the property of the author. The simple solution for this goes back to your terms of service that users must agree to when posting on your Web site or blog. They must agree that they surrender rights to anything published on your Web site or blog and that you have the right to modify or delete content as you see appropriate. Having this agreement in your terms of service protects you. Without this, you may tread into dangerous waters by modifying posts without permission of the author (or owner).

Criminal Activity

You must monitor your blogs for criminal activity in accordance with the Communications Decency Act. You may be protected under Section 230 for libelous or slanderous comments; however, you are not protected from criminal activity or intellectual property violations. Intellectual property violations may be things such as distributing copyright music or DVDs. If you allow criminal activity on your Web site or your blog, you are subject to prosecution. Bottom line: Do not allow it and delete it when and if it is posted on your blogs.

Using Images

Unless you own an image or it is royalty-free, you should not post it. A common practice is to "grab" images from other pages and use them on your own site or blog. Copyright infringement occurs whenever copyrighted material is transferred to or from a Web site without authorization from the copyright owner;

this applies to content and images. Transferring information to and from a Web site can be done in several ways. You can take information from a Web site by copying or downloading. Material can be uploaded from your computer to a Web server, or you can use an inline link to "pull" the image into your Web site or blog by calling that image URL but not physically pulling the image file onto your blog or Web server. As part of your terms of service, include that you retain the right to modify content to remove linking or copyright images.

Fair use may also come into play in regard to the use of images and material in your blog. Wikipedia.org states that fair use is defined as a "doctrine in United States copyright law that allows limited use of copyrighted material without requiring permission from the rights holders, such as use for scholarship or review. It provides for the legal, non-licensed citation or incorporation of copyrighted material in another author's work under a four-factor balancing test. It is based on free speech rights provided by the First Amendment to the United States Constitution." A good source for interpreting copyright and fair use may be found at the Franklin Pierce Law Center at **http://www.piercelaw.edu/ tfield/copynet.htm.**

This chapter merely scratches the surface of the foggy and ever-changing legalities surrounding blogging.

Chapter 11

Introduction to RSS Feeds, Atom, and Syndication

We have already discussed RSS and Atom feeds. Now we will take a closer look at syndication, how RSS/Atom feeds work, and how they exponentially expand your blog's overall effectiveness.

Wikipedia states that "RSS (which, in its latest format, stands for Really Simple Syndication) is a family of Web feed formats used to publish frequently updated content such as blog entries, news headlines, or podcasts. An RSS document, which is called a 'feed,' 'Web feed,' or 'channel,' contains either a summary of content from an associated Web site or the full text. RSS makes it possible for people to keep up with their favorite Web sites in an automated manner that's easier than checking them manually."

RSS gives you an easy way to syndicate your blogs to your readers. An RSS feed provides your readers with all recent content posted to your blog, with links to each content page. By subscribing to an RSS feed, your customers are automatically notified whenever new content is posted.

According to Blogger.com, Atom is "one name for two things: It's both a new standard for developers, as well as a syndication format or 'feed' for your blog. When a regularly updated site such as a blog has a feed, people can subscribe to it using software for reading syndicated content called a 'newsreader.' People like using readers for blogs because it allows them to catch up on all their favorites at once. Like checking e-mail — without the SPAM."

RSS- and Atom-powered blogs are the most effective way to keep the lines of communication open with your audience and support your goals, such as customer interaction, acquiring new customers, improving customer relations, selling products, or promoting your goods, services, or business/organizational philosophy.

As you know, e-mail can be time-consuming, ineffective, and challenging due to spam blockers and filters, which prevent even legitimate subscriber e-mails from reaching their intended targets. Syndication removes these obstacles helps you generate new business by effectively marketing directly to your subscribers.

The great part is that both of the free blog applications we have previewed (Blogger and WordPress) automatically include the capability to create RSS or Atom feeds.

The concept is very simple. You publish blog posts on a regular basis and people want to read your blog posts. As you publish blog posts, they appear on your blog; however, in addition they are sent out in an XML-formatted file (RSS or Atom) to your subscriber or syndication list, and they are automatically delivered to readers.

Typically, a "reader" is an e-mail application or built into the Web browser (or you can download a free reader — this blog has a great listing: **http://blogspace.com/rss/readers**). Then, as you publish new posts, they are automatically sent to the subscribers. The subscribers then open your feed in their reader and browse your new blog posts. They do not even need to be online to do this. A perfect example is for an individual who travels often for work or pleasure. They subscribe to various blog RSS or Atom feeds, and the information is pushed to them as soon as it is published. They can then browse, read, and reply to these new blog posts offline and maximize the use of their time when they do not have Internet connectivity.

With RSS or Atom there is no spam, no viruses, no phishing, no identify theft, no opt-out process that may or may not be functional. They are safe and simple to establish, send and receive.

Creating an RSS Feed in WordPress

Establishing an RSS feed with WordPress is simple. Navigate to your Dashboard and click on the "Presentation" link, and then click on the widgets tab. Drag one of the "text" widgets to your sidebar and double click on the blue lines in the text box to open the parameters feature.

In the parameters you simply enter your title and your RSS link in the format below. Replace yourblog.wordpress.com with your actual blog address, such as atlanticpub.wordpress.com and also replace "imagelocation" with the location of your RSS image icon (you should upload this image to your Web server):

```
<a href="http://yourblog.wordpress.com/feed"> <img src="http://www.
imagelocation.com/rss.png">
```

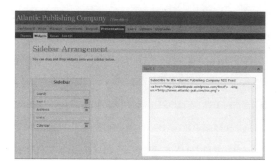

When saved, your RSS syndication feed is now displayed on your blog, as shown in the image below:

When someone clicks on this link, they will be presented with the subscription form, options on how to subscribe to the feed, and a listing of recent blog posts.

Creating an Atom Feed in Blogger

To create the Atom feed in Blogger, simply log into your Blogger dashboard. Click on "Settings," then "Site Feed." Here, you can turn your site feed to off, short (first 255 characters), or full, which is your complete blog post. With new Blogger accounts and templates, your feed is automatically displayed on your blog unless you have chosen to turn it off. If you have turned it on but are not seeing it displayed in your blog, follow the manual procedures located at **http://help.blogger.com/bin/answer. py?answer=42663**.

Microsoft provides a nice guide for how to set up an RSS feed in Outlook, which is available at **http://office.microsoft.com/en-us/ outlook/HA101595391033.asp**. Also, if you are using Microsoft Internet Explorer 7 or Firefox 2.0, it will automatically detect and notify you of any feeds available on the Web pages you are browsing. If you want to offer your RSS feed through a variety of free readers, check out **http://www.toprankblog.com/tools/rss-buttons/**, which creates buttons automatically for you to place on your Web site.

FeedBurner

As you read the expert advice throughout this book, you will notice that Feedburner is often recommended. According to FeedBurner's site, it "offers the largest feed and blog advertising network that brings together an unprecedented caliber of content aggregated from the world's most recognized media companies (e.g. Wall Street Journal Online, Wired News, Ziff Davis), A-list bloggers and blog networks and individual publishers from around the world".

There is a free version of Feedburner and a professional version that you must pay for. We will discuss the free option. Feedburner's site says it can "publicize your content and make it easy for people to subscribe; optimize distribution so that your content is properly formatted for all of the major directories and can be consumed by subscribers wherever they are; analyze your traffic to learn how many subscribers you have, where they're coming from and what they like best."

To use Feedburner, you simply type in your blog URL and follow the prompts. You set up your feed and it provides you with your Feedburner URL. You can enable some tracking and statistics options on your feed and you can add the code to your blog. It provides a step-by-step walkthrough for Blogger, and you can add the code as a text widget in WordPress. If you upgrade to the full self-hosted version of WordPress, a plugin is available to simplify the process.

One of the nice features of Feedburner is the statistics. It also presents the subscriber with a variety of options as far as which reader to choose from. Feedburner is an excellent application, and I highly recommend you replace your default Blogger and WordPress RSS/Atom feeds with your Feedburner feeds.

This chapter provided you with much more detail on how to establish an RSS or Atom feed. There is no reason not to create the feed, as it will grow your audience base, allow you to consistently send all blog posts to your subscribers, and the best part is the process is completely automated, seamless, and free.

Chapter 12

How to Make Money with Blogging

Aside from the traffic and revenue increases that you can realize by establishing a blog and following the principles in this book, what else can you do to earn more money with your blog? Attaining the aforementioned results is most likely where you will get the best returns for your time and energy; however, there are other avenues you may explore to earn money from your blog.

Google AdSense and Your Blog

Google AdSense lets you place Google advertisements on your Web pages or blogs, earning money for each click by site visitors. There are dozens of books published about Google AdSense, and most claim if you implement Google AdSense correctly you can just sit back and watch the profits roll in. I am not convinced that this was ever the case, and recently Google has changed the terms and conditions of AdSense, placing stricter limitations on the revenue potential. That said, it is a proven alternative income stream that can generate some revenue through your blog or Web site. I fully support the use of Google AdSense, and I think it is a great application; however, you need to recognize this as merely supplemental income of an unknown amount, which you are trading off for hosting advertisements on your site or blog. Contrary to some claims, you will not be able to retire or become a self-made millionaire simply by putting Google AdSense on your Web site or blog.

The concept of Google AdSense is very simple: You earn revenue potential by displaying Google ads on your Web site or in your blogs. Essentially, you become the host site for someone else's pay-per-click advertising. Since Google puts relevant CPC (cost-per-click) and CPM (cost per thousand impressions) ads through the same auction and lets them compete against one another, the auction for the advertisement takes place instantaneously, and Google AdSense subsequently displays a text or image ad(s) that will generate the maximum revenue for you.

You must choose an advertisement category to ensure only relevant, targeted advertisements appear on your Web site or blog. Google has ads for all categories of businesses and for practically all types of content, no matter how broad or specialized. The AdSense program represents advertisers ranging from large global brands to small and local companies. Ads are also targeted by geography, so global businesses can display local advertising with no additional effort. Google AdSense also supports multiple languages.

You can also earn revenue for your business by placing a Google search box on your Web site – literally paying you for search results. This service may help keep traffic on your site longer since site visitors can search directly from your site, and is also available to you at no cost, and is very simple to implement.

Google states that their "ad review process ensures that the ads you serve are not only family-friendly, but also comply with our strict editorial guidelines. We combine sensitive language filters, your input, and a team of linguists with good hard common sense to automatically filter out ads that may be inappropriate for your content." Additionally you can customize the appearance of your ads, choosing from a wide range of colors and templates. This is also the case with Google's search results page. To track your revenue, Google provides you with an arsenal of tools to track your advertising campaign and revenue.

How to Set Up Your Google AdSense Campaign

The first step is to complete the simple application form, which can be found at: **https://www.google.com/AdSense/g-app-single-1**. It is critical that you carefully review the terms of service. In particular, you must agree that you will:

- Not click on the Google ads you are serving through AdSense

- Not place ads on sites that include incentives to click on ads

In other words, you cannot click on your ads, have others click on your ads, or place text on your Web site asking anyone to click on your advertisements. The reason for this is simple — Google does not want you to generate revenue by clicking on your own ads.

When your Web site is reviewed and your account is approved, you will receive an e-mail like the one on the following pages.

GOOGLE ADSENSE E-MAIL

Your Google AdSense application has been approved. You can now activate your account and start displaying Google ads and AdSense for search on your site in minutes.

To quickly set up your account, follow the steps below. Or, for a detailed video walkthrough, view our Getting Started tutorial:

http://www.google.com/AdSensewelcome_getstarteddemo.

STEP 1: Log in to your account.

Visit **https://www.google.com/AdSense?hl=en_US** and log in using the 'Existing Customer Login' box at the top right. If you've forgotten your password, visit **https://www.google.com/AdSense/assistlogin** for assistance.

STEP 2: Generate and implement the AdSense code.

Click on the 'AdSense Setup' tab, then follow the guided steps to customize your code. When you've reached the final step, copy the code from the 'Your AdSense code' box and paste it into the HTML source of your site. If you don't have access to edit the HTML source of your pages, contact your webmaster or hosting company.

Not sure how to add the code to the HTML source of your page? Our Help with Ad Code video tutorial can guide you through the process - find the tutorial at **http://www.google.com/AdSensewelcome_implementingadcode**.

Once the code is implemented on your site, Google ads and AdSense for search will typically begin running within minutes. However, if Google has not yet crawled your site, you may not notice relevant ads for up to 48 hours.

Step 3: See the results.

After your ads start running, you can see your earnings at anytime by checking the online reports on the Reports tab in your account. For a quick overview of your earnings reports and the 5 steps to getting paid, view our Payments Guide: **https://www.google.com/AdSense/payments.**

GOOGLE ADSENSE E-MAIL

Have any questions? The AdSense Help Center is full of useful information and resources to help you familiarize yourself with.

AdSense: **https://www.google.com/support/AdSense?hl=en_US**. You can also find the latest news and tips on the AdSense blog:

http://www.AdSense.blogspot.com.

IMPORTANT NOTES:

* Want to test your ads? Please don't click on them - clicking on your own ads is against the AdSense program policies (**https://www.google.com/adsguide/policies**). Instead, try the AdSense preview tool, which allows you to check the destination of ads on your page without the risk of invalid clicks. For additional information, or to download the AdSense preview tool, please visit **https://www.google.com/support/AdSense/bin/topic.py?topic=160**.

* You can add the code to a new page or site at any time. Please keep in mind, however, that we monitor all of the web pages that contain the AdSense code. If we find that a publisher's web pages violate our policies, we'll take appropriate actions, which may include the disabling of the account. For more information, please review the Google AdSense Terms and Conditions (**www.google.com/adsguide/tnc**).

Welcome to Google AdSense. We look forward to helping you unleash the full potential of your website.

Sincerely,

The Google AdSense Team"

Google AdSense Program Policies

Since a successful Google AdSense campaign must be in compliance with all the program policies, we have reproduced them here.

To uphold the quality and reputation of Google AdSense, all publishers who apply are reviewed according to these policies.

You may notice that some policies are only relevant to publishers who have elected to receive certain Google services. For example, references to "search box" only apply to publishers who have elected to receive Google search services, and policies regarding the placement of Google ads on a site are only relevant to publishers who have elected to receive contextual ads. Please read the policies carefully and assume that they all apply to you, unless the specific policy explicitly states otherwise.

Please note that we may change our policies at any time, and pursuant to our Terms and Conditions, it is your responsibility to keep up-to-date with and adhere to the policies posted here.

Account Transferability

AdSense accounts are not transferable, assignable or resalable in connection with the sale of your site or otherwise. For example, when a site changes ownership or management, the prior owner or manager must cancel the AdSense account for the site, and the new owner or manager may sign up for a new AdSense account in his or her own name.

Ad Placement

- Up to three ad units may be displayed on each Web site page.

- A maximum of two Google AdSense for search boxes may be placed on a page.

- A single link unit may be placed on each Web site page, in addition to the ad units and search boxes specified above. Link units are considered to be 'Google ads' for purposes of these program policies.

- A single referral button per product may be placed on a page up to a maximum of 4 buttons, in addition to the ad units, search boxes, and link units specified above. Referral buttons are considered to be 'Google ads' for purposes of these program policies.

- No Google ad may be placed on any non-content-based pages.

- No Google ad or Google search box may be displayed on any domain parking websites, pop-ups, pop-unders, or in any e-mail.

- No Google ad may be placed on pages published specifically for the purpose of showing ads, whether or not the page content is relevant.

- Elements on a page must not obscure any portion of the ads, and the ad colors must be such that any ad elements, including text and URL, are visible.

- Clicks on Google ads must not result in a new browser window being launched.

Alternate Ads

If you have elected to receive contextually-targeted ads, you can make sure that your advertising space is always being used effectively, either by targeted Google ads, or by your own choice of content by specifying an image or ad server of your choice. However, you may not specify Google ads as your alternate ads.

Client Software

A site or third party cannot display our ads, search box, search results, or referral buttons as a result of the actions of any software application such as a toolbar. No Google ad, search box, or referral code may be pasted into any software application. Web pages displaying our ads, search box, search results, or referral buttons may not be loaded by any software that can trigger pop-ups, redirect users to unwanted websites, modify browser settings, or otherwise interfere with site navigation. It is your responsibility to ensure that no ad network or affiliate uses such methods to direct traffic to pages that contain your AdSense code. Accounts involved in this type of activity may be permanently disabled.

Code Modification

Any AdSense ad code, search box code, or referral code must be pasted directly into Web pages without modification. AdSense participants are not allowed to alter any portion of the ad code or change the layout, behavior, targeting, or delivery of ads for any reason.

Competitive Ads and Services

We do not permit Google ads or search boxes accessing Google search services to be published on web pages that also contain what could be considered competing ads or services. If you have elected to receive contextually-targeted Google ads, this would include all other contextually-targeted ads or links on the same page as Google ads. This would also include ads throughout the site that mimic Google ads or otherwise appear to be associated with Google on your site. Although you may sell ads directly on your site, it is your responsibility to ensure these ads do not mimic Google ads. If you have elected to receive Google search services, this would include other search services on the same site and non-Google query-targeted ads. We do allow affiliate or limited-text links.

Copyrighted Material

In order to avoid associations with copyright claims, website publishers may not display Google ads on web pages with MP3, Video, News Groups, and Image Results.

Dialers

Your site must not require or prompt an end user to download a dialer in order to view content of the site.

Incentives

Web pages may not include incentives of any kind for users to click on ads. This includes encouraging users to click on the ads or to visit the advertisers' sites as well as drawing any undue attention to the ads. For example, your site cannot contain phrases such as "click here," "support us," "visit these links," or other similar language that could apply to any ad, regardless of content. These activities are strictly prohibited in order to avoid potential inflation of advertiser costs. In addition, publishers may not bring unnatural attention to sites displaying ads or referral buttons through unsolicited mass emails or unwanted advertisements on third-party websites. Publishers are also not permitted to use deceptive or unnatural means to draw attention to or incite clicks on referral buttons.

Labeling Ads

Publishers may not label the ads with text other than "sponsored links" or "advertisements." This includes any text directly above our ads that could be confused with, or attempt to be associated with Google ads.

Language

The AdSense ad code for contextually-targeted ads may be placed on pages with content primarily in any of our supported languages. Ads must not be displayed on any page with content primarily in an unsupported language.

Prohibited Clicks and Impressions

Any method that artificially generates clicks or impressions is strictly prohibited. These prohibited methods include but are not limited to: repeated manual clicks or impressions, incentives to click or to generate impressions, using robots, automated click and impression generating tools, third-party services that generate clicks or impressions such as paid-to-click, paid-to-surf, autosurf, and click-exchange programs, or any deceptive software. Please note that clicking on your own ads for any reason is prohibited, to avoid potential inflation of advertiser costs.

Site may not include:

- Excessive profanity

- Violence, racial intolerance, or advocate against any individual, group, or organization

- Hacking/cracking content

- Illicit drugs and drug paraphernalia

- Pornography, adult, or mature content

- Gambling or casino-related content

- Excessive advertising

- Any other content that promotes illegal activity or infringes on the legal rights of others

- Pop-ups, pop-unders or exit windows that interfere with site navigation, obscure Google ads, change user preferences, or are for downloads. Other types of pop-ups, pop-unders, or exit windows may be allowed, provided that they do not exceed a combined total of 5 per user session

- Excessive, repetitive, or irrelevant keywords in the content or code of web pages

- Deceptive or manipulative content or construction to improve your site's search engine ranking, e.g., your site's PageRank

- Incentives (monetary or point-based) to users or third-party beneficiaries for online activity including, but not limited to, clicking on ads or links, performing searches, surfing websites, reading emails, or completing surveys

- Sales or promotion of certain weapons, such as firearms, ammunition, balisongs, butterfly knives, and brass knuckles

- Sales or promotion of beer or hard alcohol

- Sales or promotion of tobacco or tobacco-related products

- Sales or promotion of prescription drugs

- Sales or promotion of products that are replicas or imitations of designer goods

Site Functionality

Your site must not contain broken links and must be launched, functioning, and easily navigable.

Site Responsiveness

Sites must respond adequately to support requests and enquiries of their users.

Webmaster Guidelines

In addition to the standards above, AdSense participants are required to adhere to the webmaster guidelines posted at **http://www.google.com/webmasters/guidelines.html**. Some relevant items from the guidelines are included below for your reference:

- Do not load pages with irrelevant or excessive key words.

- Do not employ cloaking or sneaky redirects.

- Do not create multiple pages, subdomains, or domains with substantially duplicate content.

- Avoid hidden text or hidden links.

- Keep the links on a given page to a reasonable number (fewer than 100).

- Do not participate in link schemes designed to increase your site's ranking or PageRank. In particular, avoid links to web spammers or "bad neighborhoods" on the web as your website may be affected adversely by those links."

Setting Up AdSense on Your Web Site

When you first sign into your account, you will see the "Today's Earning" text, along with any action notices, such as the one in the screen shot to release payment. To set up your initial AdSense account, click on the "My Account" tab. Be aware that, because Google will be paying you, you will be required to complete several steps before your account is activated, such as provide W-9 tax data and choose your form of payment (electronic transfer or check payment).

Click on the "Account Setup" to begin setting up your advertisements. Choose which product you would like to add to your Web site. You may choose either AdSense for Content, AdSense for Search, or Referrals, then choose your Ad Type. You will be presented with more options to choose from, including unit format, colors, and other options. Choose your desired options using the drop-down menus. (Note: This is not the actual advertisement that will be displayed on your Web site, but merely a sample of how it may appear.)

You may use the "More Options" link to enable Custom Channels or elect to alternate ads or colors, including the option to show public service ads if there is no advertisement ready to be displayed on your Web site. Google states that is "common for publishers to report significant increases in revenue from changing factors like ad formats, color palettes, and placement — increases you can track with channels. Channels offer a deeper level of analysis than that provided by overall revenue reports. They allow you to break down reporting to monitor the performance of sites, sections of sites, or even individual ad units. Any time a channel is created, AdSense will record impressions, CTR, CPM, and earnings statistics for that specific page or ad unit. This provides you with a precise method of evaluating which sites and which locations will enable you to realize your maximum earning potential."

After choosing your selections, you will be provided with HTML code that simply needs to be placed in the HTML code on your Web site. You are free to place the code on one or many Web pages within your site.

When you insert the HTML code into your Web site, your campaign is activated and advertisements are immediately served to your site. Remember: Do not click on your advertisement at any time, even to "test" them. Google provides a preview mode for testing.

Hints and Tips for Maximizing Google AdSense

Use these hints and tips to maximize your earning potential:

- Always follow the Google AdSense Guidelines.

- Do not modify or change the Google AdSense HTML code you place on your Web site.

- Do not use colored backgrounds on the Google AdSense ads. If you have a Web site with a colored background, modify the advertisement to match your background.

- Place your ads so they are visible. If someone needs to scroll down to see your ads, you will likely not get any clicks on them. Play with the placement to maximize visibility.

- Do not include incentives for anyone to click on your ads (i.e., click here, click on my ads, etc.). This is also a violation of the Google AdSense guidelines. Do not have friends, family, or co-workers click on the advertisements.

- Do not click on your own ads. Do not reload your browser and click on your ads and do not test your ads out by clicking on them.

- Do not place ads in pop-up windows.

- Do not buy an "AdSense Template Web Site," which is readily available on eBay and other online marketplaces. These "get rich click" campaigns are against Google's policies and do not make money.

- Text ads typically do better than image ads. If you insist on image ads, keep them reasonable. I recommend only using the 300x250 medium rectangle.

- You can modify the URL link color in the advertisement through the Google AdSense account panel. This makes it stand out and attracts the eye of the site visitor.

- If your Web site has articles on it that you wish to embed advertisements in, use these guidelines: For short articles place the ad above the article; for long articles embed it within the content of the article.

- Wider format advertisements are more successful.

- Distribute ads on each Web page. Combine ads with referrals and search boxes so your blog does not look like a giant billboard.

- Put the Google search box near the top right hand corner of your page.

- If your advertisement is based on content, the first lines of the page determine your site content for ad serving purposes.

- Set the Google AdSense search box results window so that it opens in a new window. This prevents people from navigating away from your site.

Paid Blogging

This is a very controversial subject. If you are a company, organization, or cause that wants to jump start your blog traffic, you can hire bloggers to publish posts on it. Or, if you want to earn some money by blogging, this is a potential source of revenue for you. In short, companies will pay you (the blogger) to do what you do best — blog. The catch is that you must write about products, services, Web sites, and companies in a positive manner. Do your blog posts truly reflect your "real" opinions about the products, services, Web sites, companies you are blogging about in such a glowing review? Well, it does not really matter; you are getting paid for doing so. Therein lies the controversy. Respected bloggers can lose their reputations when they blog for cash. To be fair, most pay-for-blogging services state that you pick what you want to blog on and are free to post whatever you want about the topic (within the terms of service) and some require disclosure. Disclosure simply means that your blog posts will reveal to others that you are getting paid for the blog post.

Let us look at the top four pay-for-blogging sites:

- PayPerPost.com (**www.payperpost.com**): Claims that you can "Get paid for blogging. You've been writing about Web sites, products, services and companies you love for years and you have yet to benefit from all the sales and traffic you have helped generate. That's about to change. With PayPerPost advertisers are willing to pay you for your opinion on various topics. Search through a list of Opportunities, make a blog posting, get your content approved, and get paid. It's that simple."

Who pays for this blogging? The answer is advertisers. The easy way to generate traffic on your blog is to pay bloggers to publish positive posts about your company, products, or services. You can earn as much as $20 for a blog post. PayPerPost does require disclosure.

- Blogvertise (**www.blogvertise.com**): Blogvertise claims that "Our Advertisers want YOU to mention and talk about their websites products and services in your blogs and journals. They want the publicity, the exposure, the Buzz! that online bloggers and internet journals can generate for their web site products and services. In exchange blogsvertise pays YOU in paypal per task/blog entry, for writing / talking about / mentioning their website in your blog!" Blogvertise is unique in that the advertisers may actually select the bloggers they want to blog about their products or services. You are told what products or service to write about in your blog and can earn $4 to $25 per blog entry. Your blog is required to be at least 60 to 100 words and contain a minimum of three or more links. Endorsing the Web site product or service is not a requirement.

- ReviewMe (**www.reviewme.com**): Reviewme.com is like a combination of the previous two services. Advertisers pay a $10 flat fee per review and have the option to select specific bloggers for a premium. Reviewme.com pays bloggers between $20 and $200 for each review. You must submit an application and get accepted to be eligible as a participating blogger.

- CREAMaid (**www.creamaid.com**): CREAMaid states that it "is a service that lets you meet other bloggers with similar interests, and make money while doing it." You create a CREAMaid conversation widget and insert it into your blog post. Your post is now eligible to be "selected." Once selected, it is syndicated to all participating posts throughout the network and, when selected, you receive a payment. In essence, advertisers create a "conversation widget." The conversation widget tells you what topic to write about. You must accept it and write about the topic in a post. If the advertiser selects your post, it is incorporated in participating blogs across the network. Since the advertiser selects which blog posts to use, you might want to make sure they are complimentary.

As a business, organization, or cause, you will likely find yourself on the advertiser side of the table; however, if you have plenty of free time and like to blog, this is a potential source of revenue for you. One key factor is that you must qualify. While qualification terms vary, most require you to have a well-established, quality blog with significant posts (i.e., you need to be a very established and reputable blogger for your opinion to be of value). Do some research and you will find there are dozens of other pay-for-blogging Web sites, all with differing terms and conditions.

EARN CASH FROM BLOGGING

By Smorty.COM

Blog advertising has only recently been understood by the larger SEO and Web advertising community as a way to generate traffic and increase rankings for advertisers. With traffic and rankings being the number one need for online merchants, it's great news for bloggers wanting to make some extra cash from their active blogs.

Blogs only become successful by their content. Whether they have an active readership or just rank highly for the keywords they use, it's the content which in turn brings the money in one form or another. Since advertising banners and AdSense can really turn off readers and often won't generate the kind of money a blogger can live on, it looks like it is good old-fashioned work which is going to bring in the dollars.

Blog advertising is when an advertiser pays a blogger to write an opinion article about their products and services with a backlink on a keyword of choice. The blogger must research the advertisers' site and their article must be descriptive and unique. This will generally only take 10 minutes for the blogger to write; however, the payment for this work can range from $5 to sometimes $100. The content not only helps bring the advertiser traffic but also helps the blogger build a unique content- rich blog which will start to rank higher in search engines, often bring a higher pagerank and often higher paying jobs from advertisers, a win-win situation. This win-win is why there is such a great future in blog advertising.

Advertisers will always need instant traffic and bloggers have instant readers. It's in the best interest of bloggers to write positive articles about an advertisers' service and store it permanently on their blog. So now you have a permanent, uniquely written advertisement bringing a constant stream of visitors with better search engine rankings from the backlink and a happy blogger with money in their pocket with a content-rich blog bringing more and more visitors each post.

Smorty is a blog advertising company. We focus on building a network of the highest quality blogs rather than a large network of poor quality blogs. This brings our advertisers a better result for their search engine rankings and traffic, in other words, a better result for their money. For more details, visit http://www.smorty.com.

BRIBING BLOGGERS AND ADVERTISING IN BLOGS

By Meryl K. Evans

The blogosphere has been abuzz with the news about bloggers who received a PC loaded with Vista from Microsoft. The company told the bloggers they could keep the PCs, donate them, or return them. Here's an entry from Joel on the topic.

Sites like PayPerPost and Blogitive pay bloggers to mention a product or service in their entries. The site encourages bloggers to disclose their relationship with PayPerPost, but it's not required. I am not getting paid to mention these two companies. However, I've posted ads for Blogitive before its site went up and have yet to accept an offer from its site. I also registered with PayPerPost when it was first announced, and haven't taken advantage of it.

After that experience, I'm less inclined to do that sort of advertising again as I don't like it that some of my blog entries have crazy keywords in them. I also acknowledged they were ads by stating, "From the sponsor."

How do you find a balance between earning money to support non-paying activities and turning off readers? These experiments taught me to limit site sponsorship and avoid regularly posting ads within my blog entries (aside from Google's), although I did add a new sponsor yesterday to an old post. She approached me and the site met my requirements, so I accepted the offer. My two rules: Honesty and Selectivity.

You may not agree with what I do, but I'm honest about it. I don't like in your face or deceptive advertising and keep that in mind with this site. Only the blogs contain the advertising with the exception of the sponsors on the sidebar — those appear on most pages. Over time, I've gotten more stringent (here's the selective part) about what ads or sponsors I accept. If you find any of the current ones unacceptable, they're from before I changed my rules. Out of respect for the folks behind them, I let them continue sponsorship.

Reviews are different. Some of them come from stuff I bought and others from free copies. Free or not — the reader is my first priority when writing a review. When I read reviews, I want honest feedback about the product or service, and I provide the same. These aren't pricey items like a laptop — usually books or games. I've turned down review opportunities because the product wasn't good quality (rather turn it down than waste my time and write a bad review) or the topic had nothing to do with anything I ever write about — applying the selectivity rule.

BRIBING BLOGGERS AND ADVERTISING IN BLOGS

Meryl K. Evans, Content Maven behind meryl.net, is Editor-in-Chief of Shavlik's The Remediator Security Digest, a popular newsletter on computer security with over 100,000 subscribers. She's also the editor of Professional Service Journal, an e-mail newsletter for business-to-business service providers, Intel Solution Services' Connected Digest, and TailoredMail's Focus eJournal. Meryl is an educator with New York University's online graduate program. She has worked for two Fortune 500 telecom companies, the U.S. federal government in Washington, D.C., and does IT consulting.

Chapter 13

The Future of the Blog

Blogging is here for the long haul. It is incredibly easy, free, and available to large corporations, as well as teens who blog about the trials and tribulations of life. Blogging is powerful and has moved out of the closet into mainstream culture. The blog has been directly responsible for breaking some significant news events, such as the debacle with Dan Rather and President Bush's service record to revealing intimate secrets of the Hollywood elite. Their business impact, while not glorified in the evening news, has been significant, and there is a direct correlation between effective blogs and increased business communications, product awareness, Web site traffic, and revenue increases.

All is not perfect in the blogosphere though. Recent landmark libel and slander cases against bloggers have proven that you cannot say whatever you want, whenever you want, about whomever you want. I believe there will be more legal decisions that affect blogging, and while the lines between what you can and cannot do will become more clearly defined, just as with e-mail and the CAN-SPAM Act of 2003, the list of what you cannot do and the penalties for breaking the law will also be clearly defined and harsh.

Questions still abound as to what protection bloggers should have. Are they journalists? What are the standards? What is the real responsibility of the blog owner to manage the user-defined content on his blog? What are the privacy law requirements and disclosure laws? How has pay-for-blogging corrupted the sanctity of blogging – or has it? Lots of questions, few answers, but over time, each will be addressed and answered.

When I first started researching this book, I sent out information to many blogging businesses, businesses that use blogs and bloggers, asking for their input and advice for the book. I got a very mixed response. There is a large group of self-proclaimed blogmasters who feel only they are the true artists of blogging, and every else is a poser. The laughable part is most of these bloggers have not accepted the reality that blogging has grown beyond the teenage diary days, and corporate America has embraced blogging for the long haul. On the other hand, there are many individuals and businesses who specialize in blogging and are truly masters of establishing blogs for businesses and organizations and can help get your blog up and running quickly, integrate it with your Web site, and manage the overall process. You will find I have highlighted many of them in this book. Other bloggers are truly recognized as masters of the art of blogging and have taken very proactive stances on legal issues, as well as the practice of pay-for-blogging. Pay-for-blogging, while great for those who make money from it, is truly one of the biggest challenges for the future of blogging. If you are being paid to blog about a product, service, or company, how much faith can we take in what you are saying? The sanctity and innocence of the blogosphere has been damaged and will continue to be damaged. I salute those companies who force disclosure so at least you know when you are reading paid blog posts.

Your company will have a personality through its blogs. Employees and customers can interact with each other, share information, address concerns, and help you grow your customer base. I mentioned early in this book that blogging is not just for external communication. Businesses have successfully used blogs behind corporate firewalls for internal communications, collaboration, information sharing, context management, content management, and project management. I think you will see a growth in the use of internal blogs, as well as an explosion in the business adaptation and use of content management systems, such as ExpressionEngine.

Over time, the face of blogging will change, and new laws will both protect and most likely provide new opportunities for the prosecution of bloggers. Proposed anti-blogging legislation is on the rise, and settlements against bloggers have been awarded.

The issue of protection under the First Amendment's freedom of the press still needs to be defined, if there is any protection afforded to bloggers at all. Clearly, not all bloggers are journalists by trade, but then again some are, and bloggers do perform similar functions to journalists, so maybe they are journalists. How do we decide? I think this is an issue the justice system will eventually decide, and it will affect the future of blogging.

The bottom line is blogging is here to stay and will continue to grow in popularity and professionalism. Businesses and organizations will continue to adopt and implement blogs as part of their overall business plans, and the skill level of corporate bloggers will grow. Blogging will replace e-mail as the way to engage customers about products and services. You can be confident that your investment in blogging is good for the long haul, and it will be an invaluable tool for your business, organization, or cause.

Chapter 14

Summary

When I was approached to write this book, I jumped at the opportunity. If you have read my biography, you know that I am a Lieutenant Commander in the United States Coast Guard, and my interest in computer hardware, Web design, and Web development grew out of a simple desire to put some photos of my children on the Web for our family to view. In my Coast Guard career, we moved often, were underway or deployed quite a bit of the time, and never stationed very close to home. Designing Web sites, starting my own business, and writing books was something I did in my spare time (and there was not much of it). Surprisingly, I did not have a blog, was not a blogger, did not design and implement blogs, and I did not know how simple yet powerful blogging could be to the small business, organization, or cause. Of the five books I have written, this was by far the most challenging yet rewarding. I learned volumes of information and hope that I have captured it for you. I liken my journey writing this book to a line from one of the best movies of all time (*The Blues Brothers*). "It's 106 miles to Chicago, we've got a full tank of gas, half a pack of cigarettes, it's dark, and we're wearing sunglasses. Hit it." I like to replace the "hit it" part with: Blog it! It sort of felt like that kind of a trip from beginning to end.

I read several books, researched for hundreds of hours, tested blog software, and interviewed many blogging professionals. As with all my previous books, I wanted a practical, fact-filled reference book that had relevant material for the small business, organization, or cause to begin designing and implementing an effective blog for free. This book was designed to be the starting point for those with limited or no budget, whose IT staff usually consisted of themselves and a few other employees who perform multiple jobs. My hope is that you will find this guide an invaluable addition to your reference library and refer to it often as you embark on your journey into the blogosphere.

As I have said in this book several times, blogging is powerful, cheap, and fun. It can be challenging, rewarding, and always enlightening. Do not underestimate the powerful voice bloggers have in effecting change. Take a look at the recent decision by Microsoft to extend the warranty on their XBOX 360 machines from one year to three. While certainly not the only reason why, customer complaints about the early demise of many XBOX 360 machines led to the decision by Microsoft, and leading the charge was the blogging community. In this case, there is no doubt: Their message was received loud and clear.

Enjoy your journey into the world of blogging!

Chapter 15

Blogging Profile, Case Studies, & Outsourcing

In this chapter, I bring you one of the most respected designers of blog or blog-powered Web sites, highlight their services and achievements through case studies, and provide insight into outsourcing your blog as an alternative to in-house blogging and blog development. I have chosen ContentRobot for their outstanding professional service and superior reputation.

ContentRobot

ContentRobot, based out of East Berlin, Connecticut, is a technology company committed to developing effectively designed and well-written business blogs and blog-powered Web sites. They enhance company Internet presences to build stronger brands, nurture client relationships, and enhance profitability.

The ContentRobot team is comprised of passionate technologists, designers, writers, and communicators who want to help you take your blogs and Web sites to the next level.

ContentRobot provides all the services businesses need to develop an effective Internet presence. They specialize in business blogs (this can mean any blog that focuses on a hobby to a full-blown corporate site or anything in between) or a blog-powered Web site. They use their vast award-winning experience to deliver results.

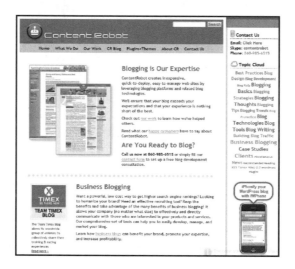

ContentRobot Case Studies

Bazaarvoice: Business Blog Design Complements Corporate Web Site

Purpose: Bazaarblog is the company blog for Bazaarvoice. This Austin, Texas, company develops outsourced technology, services, analytics, and expertise to encourage and harness word of mouth marketing and bring it closer to a company's brand and customer experience.

The blog allows Bazaarvoice to share ideas and thoughts with prospects, clients, partners, analysts, press, and marketers interested in improving online experience, conversion, and word of mouth. While Bazaarvoice had an initial blog presence, they sought ContentRobot to convert the blog from TypePad to WordPress with a new design and poise it for further growth.

Features: The WordPress platform offers Bazaarvoice a way to easily author the blog and manage comments to keep the conversation going. The new blog design stands alone, but is readily aligned with the Bazaarvoice brand.

The Bazaarblog readers can keep up with Bazaarvoice information, view Bazaarvoice's favorite Web sites and books, search for content, comment on the posts, sign-up for a newsletter, contact them with a handy form, and subscribe to the feed. On the back-end, Bazaarvoice tracks it all with Feedburner statistics and Performancing blog metrics.

Why It's Successful: This conversion of the site from TypePad to WordPress was a success. ContentRobot was able to take a basic blog, convert the existing content into the new format, and add a myriad of features so that Bazaarvoice can author and manage its new blog.

Go see: **http://www.bazaarblog.com**

Beneath the Cover / Push the Key: Content + Technology

Purpose: Michael Drew sought ContentRobot to create the Push the Key blog and soon after asked us to help him develop its complementary blog-powered Web site, Beneath the Cover. These sites discuss the ins and outs of the publishing industry. Publishers, editors, designers, authors, and literary agents alike can find an abundance of articles that will help them do their jobs.

Go to BTC to read what its expert contributors have to say and go to PTK to see the response to those opinions. These sites will continue to evolve as each offers custom newsletters and RSS feed options, designed to allow readers to target the content they wish to receive on a regular basis.

Features: A key goal of both projects was to make it easy to find and read posts in a variety of ways. ContentRobot then integrated and (heavily) customized two WordPress themes so that several contributors, 75 categories, and hundreds of articles were displayed both logically and enticingly.

Visitors can navigate the sites via the dropdown menus, which show various topics at a glance. Readers can interact by adding comments and rating stories by simply clicking on "thumbs up" or "thumbs down" buttons and can read recommended blog posts from other Internet resources that round out the vast content.

The Push the Key blog features post titles that act as a great separator between stories and can be tailored to the content. The handy topic cloud shows off the depth of the content PTK offers.

Beneath the Cover is much less bloggy as it highlights its contributors and their expertise. Due to its sheer amount of content, BTC provides featured posts and customized category pages to help visitors navigate the site.

Why It's Successful: These sites are building an impressive following with comments and interaction steadily on the increase. This initial success has attracted more contributors to write content for BTC, which makes these sites definitive resources for all things publishing.

Go see: **http://www.beneaththecover.com**
            http://www.pushthekey.com

Bite of the Best: Blog-Powered Web Site

Purpose: Bite of the Best is a tasty new blog-powered Web site that offers commentary about the "best" products you can find in your grocery stores. A true family affair, Bonnie Tandy Leblang, a nationally recognized food writer — along with her sons — write the content, while the Tandy sisters created the design. ContentRobot implemented their vision using the WordPress blog platform and related technologies.

Features: Each week, visitors can read a "featured bite" and registered users can get involved in the site by adding their two cents (via comments) and rating products they've tried. Especially fun is that these users can enter a variety of contests to win free products, which include food products and kitchen gadgets. Fans can follow the blog along in an RSS reader or a newsletter, which is delivered to their inboxes each Wednesday.

BOTB readers are treated to lively and entertaining writing. However, behind the scenes, ContentRobot customized many WordPress elements to make the site function. Among the enhancements were optimizing the taxonomy so that the Tandys can easily categorize and showcase "bites" and marketplace items. Also, to keep the post's design consistent, WordPress's custom fields properly display the "factoids" or details of each product.

This site takes advantage of many external tools, such as:

- **Amazon:** Allows readers to easily purchase products at Amazon with BOTB's affiliation

- **Feedblitz:** Readers can subscribe to a heavily customized, blog-driven newsletter, which is sent every Wednesday

- **Feedburner:** Provides feed tools and subscriber tracking

- **Google Analytics:** Site tracking tools and analysis

- **WordPress Plugins:** A variety of SEO tools and other updates were installed

- **Wufoo:** Allows BOTB to effortlessly create online forms and allows readers to enter contests

Why It's Successful: Bite of the Best is able to easily publish interesting content for its readers and provide a great place for food manufacturers to promote their products. The number of subscribers continues to rise on this new blog-powered Web site. Building on its success, BOTB will be offering even more for its readers, including recipes.

Go see: **http://www.biteofthebest.com**

GrokDotCom: Newsletter to Blog Conversion

Purpose: GrokDotCom, published by the Conversion Rate Specialists, Future Now, is an award-winning newsletter that contains plain spoken and refreshingly irreverent content that helps their clients develop and maintain Web sites that persuade their visitors to act.

Future Now wanted to convert its existing newsletter, which resided on a proprietary software, and Movable type blog onto the more flexible WordPress blog platform. Now GrokDotCom features articles and posts written by Future Now authors, along with an extensive "blended" RSS feed of industry news.

Readers can learn more about online conversion rates, accountable multi-channel marketing, and Web analytics by reading the blog, subscribing to it via RSS, or receiving daily, weekly, or monthly newsletter content into their e-mail inboxes.

Features: ContentRobot customized the two-column WordPress theme to display the latest articles, blog posts, announcements, and events on the home page. At a glance, visitors can click to the "Persuasion Architect" posts and check out the GrokDotCom calendar. Readers can dig deeper to the posts and interact with the Future Now experts by adding their own comments and insights.

Behind the scenes, much attention was paid to search engine optimization to get the best search engine placement for the sheer volume of content that this blog steadily publishes. ContentRobot installed and configured Tag Warrior, SEO Title Tag, and Google Sitemaps, among others.

ContentRobot also customized three newsletter templates for those readers who prefer to get the Grok content in their e-mail boxes. Each aggregates different content feeds for different timeframes (daily, weekly, and monthly).

Why It's Successful: ContentRobot was able to bring together several sources of content and pour them into a single content management system. The resulting converted site is easy to use and the content is accessible in many ways. GrokDotCom appreciates the simplicity of adding, categorizing, and tagging content in their WordPress-driven site. Sending out the newsletters, which was a time consuming and manual process, has now been mercifully automated — saving time and money to get word out to the masses.

Go see: **http://www.grokdotcom.com**

New School Selling: Blog-Powered Web Site and Newsletter

Purpose: New School Selling sought a new Web site because it was moving away from its "Sales Warrior" model toward a new branding effort, along with recently expanded products and services. To build a cost-effective, feature-laden site, ContentRobot developed the NSS Web presence using blogging software as its platform — or created a blog-powered Web site.

By implementing WordPress and a variety of plug-ins, the redesigned NSS Web site not only offers detailed information about their training courses and products, but it includes a blog and a newsletter — so that NSS's readers can stay informed about New School Selling and its offerings.

Features: Visitors can learn New School Selling's sales philosophy and why the old methods of selling either don't work or are increasingly becoming less effective.

Readers can discover (and purchase) the variety of training that NSS offers, from in-house seminars to weekly telecourses. The event calendar allows readers to see at a glance where owner Steve Clark is teaching or when the telecourses are being held. Behind the scenes, maintaining the schedule is as easy as writing a post.

Subscribers can keep track of entire blogs via an RSS newsreader. Readers not familiar with RSS, or who prefer to receive information via e-mail, can get the latest posts in their inbox by signing up for the newsletter. Existing newsletter readers were simply converted to the new blog-driven newsletter technology without disruption of their subscription.

Why It's Successful: The former flat, one-way Web site has been transformed into an interactive one, where visitors can learn about NSS and get more involved in the company. At a glance, the event calendar keeps readers up-to-date and aware of NSS happenings. The blog is where readers can get information about sales and the selling process and are encouraged to exchange ideas.

Go see: **http://www.newschoolselling.com**

Shop.org: Membership Blogging

Purpose: Shop.org is an association that is comprised of interactive executives from more than 500 nationally recognized retail brands (both big and small). They participate to share information, lessons learned, new perspectives, insights, and intelligence about online and multichannel retailing.

To extend their diverse community online, Shop.org wanted to develop a blog where their members could write about their expertise and experiences to spur lively conversation (perhaps even a bit of a debate) to uncover best practices and solutions that work.

The blog focuses on topics such as affiliate programs, analytics, IT, marketing and consumer trends, e-commerce, search engine marketing, Web 2.0, and user-generated content. All Shop.org members are encouraged to write as many stories as they wish and to comment freely on others' posts.

Features: ContentRobot designed a clean and stylish two-column WordPress theme to compliment the Shop.org logo. They also incorporated the association's primary colors (red, grey, and white) and other visual cues from the main Web site for the overall look.

The Shop.org blog's motto is "By the Member, For the Member" and this is best illustrated by prominently listing its contributors in the right column. Authors have their own RSS feeds so members can subscribe to any contributor or get the entire blog's content RSS feed as well.

ContentRobot worked closely with the Shop.org team to create blogging guidelines and specific corporate policies that detailed who can post, how comments would be handled, and how members join the blog.

Why It's Successful: Since its launch, the Shop.org members have been busy getting trained on how to blog effectively. No longer hindered by location and time, they expect greater content and discussion to be generated in 2007 and beyond.

Go see: **http://blog.shop.org**

Team Timex Blog: Athlete Blogging

Purpose: The Team Timex Blog was developed to provide a comprehensive forum for 45 blogging athletes.

Visitors can follow the athletes as they train and compete all over the world in triathlons and other events that feature biking, swimming, and running. The bloggers educate and entertain readers about life as a Timex athlete on their tours.

Features: Each Timex-sponsored athlete authors their own blog and has their own newsfeed. This way, blog subscribers can keep track of an entire blog or any one of their favorite athletes. Readers not familiar with RSS can sign up for a newsletter and get the latest posts in their inbox.

Visitors can learn all about diet and nutrition, family life, training regimens, and even injuries from the athlete's perspective. Readers can also easily see where they are racing with the calendar of events — and come back to see how the Timex racers performed with overall race results and personal race reports.

The blog uses the WordPress platform and has several supporting plugins to extend the functionality. Timex tracks it all with Feedburner and Performancing metrics.

Why It's Successful: With a minimum of training, several athletes are already publishing some great posts — even with great supporting imagery.

ContentRobot was able to work with Timex to develop a blog that is appropriate for its communication style, in addition to determining the editorial/taxonomy considerations, configuring the software, and creating a branded design.

Go see: **http://teamtimex.timexblogs.com/**

Outsourcing Versus In-House Blog Development

If want to start a blog for your small business but you do not have the expertise, time, personnel, or other resources, you should consider outsourcing part or all of its development. The pros can help you brainstorm key strategies, provide the best-in-class solutions, and fill in the gaps for any technical, design, editorial, and marketing needs for both the short term and the long haul.

Your blog team, not unlike your Web team, needs to have these common skills to build a successful blog. Is your team missing any? If so, consider getting some outside help.

Design

First impressions count. People will form an opinion on your blog in 1/20 of a second. While you can use a default template or perhaps get one for free, realize that there are limitations. Whatever approach you follow, make sure your blog's design appropriately reflects your company, brand, and mission. To create a branded template, the key skills your team needs are:

- **Photoshop expertise:** Basic graphic design skills are paramount for image creation and photo editing

- **User Interface development:** Know how to create an overall effective blog design layout (where the navigation is most effective, where to place advertising, etc.)

- **Usability:** Creating a design that is inherently usable, not just cool

- **CSS:** Working with style sheets allows you to enhance your blog's look and feel (including colors, font, and table properties) and go beyond basic blogging templates

Technical

Do you manage your Web site? Do know what FTP and MySQL are? While installing software could take five minutes, you may not have time to play resident geek to configure your blog the way you need it to work. Small businesses might not want to worry that their blog needs a database; they just want to know that they can easily post stories to their blogs. Here is what the tech team, at a minimum, should know how to do:

- **Server setup:** Knowledge of PHP, SQL, UNIX, Apache, and RSS

- **Blog setup:** Can install and configure blog software and related components (plugins, modules, and widgets)

- **Blog management:** Can administer backend functionality, such as user registration, handling comments, and RSS feeds

- **Advanced functionality:** Add and tweak blog functionality, including forums, contact forms, comments and trackbacks, newsletters, and e-commerce

- **PHP programming:** Often custom programming is required if you want to display content in a specific way other than reverse chronology

Marketing

If you build a blog, will they come? Not necessarily. Along with fantastic content, you have to know how to attract visitors (and build readership) with a variety of online and offline techniques so they keep coming back. From blog post techniques to search engine optimization and the best social networking/ Web 2.0 practices, the pros can position your blog appropriately. Your marketers will need to know:

- **Search engine optimization:** Add keywords, descriptions, and tags to your blog posts and pages

- **Search engine marketing:** Get your site listed in major search engines (Yahoo, Google) and blog directories (Technorati, Ice Rocket)

- **Blog advertising and affiliates:** Determine what programs are available (i.e., AdSense), know which ones make sense for your site, and how to effectively implement them

- **Online techniques:** Create press releases, blog commenting strategies, banner advertising campaigns, and more

- **Offline promotion methods:** Simple things like adding your blog address to your business card and your e-mail signature will help publicize your blog

The Benefits of Working with a Blog Development Company

Your blog developers can help you determine your short- and long-term goals and help you meet them. They can help you strategize technical considerations (like hosting plans) to great blog design (2- or 3-column templates) to content development (topics and categories).

Content Approach

The easiest way to build success is to create lots of killer blog posts and have lots of great ideas in the wings. The hardest part is keeping it up and not getting discouraged with the inevitable writer's block. Your blog development company can help you establish topics and offer ideas for blog growth. A blog developer can help you brainstorm topics, create an editorial calendar, and assist with any imagery and HTML needs.

Cultivate Relationships

Do you know how to build relationships with key bloggers? Do you have a link strategy? Can you establish a comments policy that encourages visitor interaction? Get some help to seek out partnerships and evangelists — it is amazing how these connections can pay off in unexpected ways.

Intangible Skills

Your blog consultant will become your best ally in maintaining your blog. They can help by staying abreast of the latest blogging techniques and technologies to make sure your blog is up-to-date, provide technical support, and be your biggest cheerleader.

Finding a Reputable Blog Vendor

There are several ways you can find a reputable blog vendor. Similar to finding a dentist, try to:

Internet Search

Enter "blogging expert" or "blog-powered Web sites" in your favorite search engine.

Friends and Colleagues

Ask anyone in your personal and professional circles if anyone has experience working with blog developers. It is great to work with someone you already know.

Referrals

See some blogs you like? Contact the company and find out who did their blog. Happy clients are always willing to share their experiences with a certain vendor.

Then check out their Web site/blog to read more about them, check out some case studies, and contact them to talk more about your project. Your initial consultation should be at no cost. Remember, too, that some vendors may not be ready to provide prices on the phone or offer packages, due to the custom work they perform.

Chapter 16

Interviews with Professional Bloggers

In this chapter I interview numerous experienced, expert bloggers. I found their guidance and insight invaluable additions to this book, and I am sure you will as well.

CASE STUDY: STEFAN MISCHOOK

www.killersites.com
www.killerphp.com

Can you describe your introduction to blogging, how you became interested, and how has it impacted you personally?

I first heard about blogging in 2001 and dismissed it as another tool for people who did not want to learn HTML. A year or so later, I realized the significance of blogging and blogging software: It was going to allow for the original vision of the Web to actually materialize, where anyone could easily get a Web site on the Web.

Blogs and the blog phenomenon made me rethink my whole approach to Web design as a Web professional: blogs, CMS, and other similar content formatting tools were the future of Web design.

From a business perspective, how do you think blogging can positively impact communications, sales, and corporate image?

Blogs offer a great way to connect with your audience/client base in an informal and personal manner. These days, traditional hard-sell tactics of marketing are quickly

CASE STUDY: STEFAN MISCHOOK

becoming dated. Now businesses have to engage with their audience. Just as a programmer can get away with wearing jeans to work, blogs allow companies to communicate with the public in a less restricted context.

What is the best advice you can give an individual or business who is considering starting a blog?

Find someone in your company who:

- Knows your products/services.

- Is fun to be around.

- Can write and communicate well.

Keep the content of the blog peripheral to your company's core. Remember the soft-sell principle and try to engage with the audience honestly.

What industry sites and blogs do you read regularly?

Mostly technology related and international news: CNN, MSNBC.

What are your favorite blog development tools or applications?

From my experience (not that I have tested every blog tool out there,) WordPress is probably the best choice out there today because it is:

- Mature — clean code and refined functionality

- The WordPress community is big — lots of resources

Can you name five tips for successful blogging?

- Be honest.

- Be sincere.

- Keep the writing on topic.

- Keep the writing concise — people are impatient on the Web.

- Be regular with your articles.

CASE STUDY: STEFAN MISCHOOK

Can you name five common mistakes in blogging?

The opposite of the above five tips.

What is the best way to get a new blog promoted?

In the real-estate world the top three rules are:

- Location

- Location

- Location

In the blogging world, the top three rules are:

- Content

- Content

- Content

If you have good content on your blog, people will talk about it and it will spread. The Web is about viral marketing.

What is the relationship between your Web site and your blogs? How are they interconnected? How does the blog expand upon your Web site?

My blog allows me to discus topics related to my core business in an editorial manner — I can be informal. In addition, the blog is a great place for me to fill in the gaps that I may have missed in the main site and it creates another contact point for my readers. Blogs provide another style of presentation that appeals to a different audience than the main site.

What do you think is the future of blogging?

I think that blogging will continue to become more and more important because of how easy they make building a site and because they provide an informal bridge between the business and the public.

Beyond text, I think that video and audio blogging are moving mainstream.

CASE STUDY: STEFAN MISCHOOK

Stefan Mischook has been developing Web sites and Web applications since 1994. Stefan has spent the last several years working on dozens of Web and multimedia projects for small business and large pharmaceutical and banking organizations. Stefan now runs several educational Web sites, including **www.killersites.com**, **www.killerphp.com**, and **www.idea22.com**.

CASE STUDY: JUSTIN PREMICK

www.aweber.com

Can you describe your introduction to blogging, how you became interested, and how has it impacted you personally?

I personally played around with blogging years ago, but didn't get into it seriously until the idea of publishing one here at AWeber came up. I'd been reading various blogs and had an idea of their usefulness, but I can say that I've learned countless times more by doing than by observing.

Its effect on me? There have been many, but the one that sticks out in my mind is that how you say something (or don't say it at all) can be just as important as what you do say. When blogging, you're writing in a conversational tone, but without the same extralingual communication that you get from talking to someone in person or even on the phone. Inflection is difficult to convey at times, and it's easy to be misunderstood.

Of course, you can't let this dissuade you, because most people will allow for this, and if there's any uncertainty it's easily sorted out through the blog's comments.

CASE STUDY: JUSTIN PREMICK

From a business perspective, how do you think blogging can positively impact communications, sales, and corporate image?

As the audiences that we try to reach become more demanding of businesses and more resistant to traditional marketing tactics, we have to find new ways to connect with them.

Blogging is a great way to do just that — it humanizes companies, putting a face on them that potential and current customers can identify with. People do business with people they trust and who they perceive to be like them, and a good blog makes it easier for potential customers to identify with a business.

What is the best advice you can give an individual or business who is considering starting a blog?

Go do it. Don't spend countless hours worrying about what you're going to say or how you want your blog to look. You can change, improve, etc. as you go, and if anyone notices, even better — you'll look (gasp!) human.

What industry sites and blogs do you read regularly?

I have more subscriptions set up in Google Reader than I should probably admit, but even among all the excellent marketing blogs out there I can say that there are a few I read regularly:

* John Jantsch's Duct Tape Marketing blog:
   http://www.ducttapemarketing.com/weblog.php

* Mark Brownlow's E-mail Marketing Reports:
   http://www.email-marketing-reports.com/iland/

* MarketingSherpa's Articles/Blog Posts:
   http://www.marketingsherpa.com

* Joe Rawlinson's Return Customer blog:
   http://www.returncustomer.com

What are your favorite blog development tools or applications?

CASE STUDY: JUSTIN PREMICK

We stick to WordPress — just about anything we need can be done with an existing WordPress plugin! We also have the benefit of having a top-notch team of developers at AWeber who can create whatever we need but can't find in the WordPress community.

Can you name five tips for successful blogging?

- Be yourself. Differentiate yourself from companies that aren't interested in talking with their users.

- Be brief. Blogs aren't the place for a dissertation. If your posts aren't to-the-point, you won't spur on much discussion.

- Invite comments and discussion. Don't take the attitude that your opinion is the only one that counts. Value your readers and they'll value you.

- Check out your readers' blogs. If they're writing about the same things as you, get involved in the discussions on their blogs and/or reference (and link to) their posts on your own blog.

- Read other blogs – they're great places to learn how you can improve your own blog!

Can you name five common mistakes in blogging?

- Posting infrequently. It's hard to build a loyal community as an absentee blogger.

- Not participating on relevant blogs. Get involved with other people's blogs by commenting and referencing their posts, and they'll likely return the favor.

- Not offering comments or not responding to comments. It's a conversation, not a lecture. If you want to talk at someone, rather than with them, just write articles. Blogs are about interacting with people, and you can't do that by making yourself inaccessible.

- Not offering a subscribe option. Don't force people to come back to your blog to see if maybe you've posted something new. Offer an RSS feed, and an e-mail subscribe option for people who aren't familiar with RSS.

CASE STUDY: JUSTIN PREMICK

- Not letting your personality shine through. People want to know there's a living, breathing someone behind your brand. Sure, you might rub some people the wrong way, but you'll find fans, too — and they're the ones you want.

What is the best way to get a new blog promoted?

I'm not sure that our experience is the most typical. We didn't really have to do much to get the blog off the ground.

We relied on word of mouth among our users. We interspersed references to the blog with our normal user and prospect communications and found that there was quite a demand for the sort of information we were providing there.

In short, we built it and they came. But of course they were already there; we just hadn't started blogging yet. Once we did, our users responded.

The two best pieces of advice I can offer someone starting a new blog are:

- Put out great content — if it's not worth reading, all the promotion in the world is pointless.

- Find other people talking about the same things, talk about what they're talking about and credit them, and get involved in their blog communities. They, and their readers, will check your blog out, too.

What is the relationship between your Web site and your blogs? How are they interconnected? How does the blog expand upon your Web site?

The blog is our primary tool for producing and disseminating e-mail marketing advice, ideas, case studies, and commentary. We not only link to it on our main page, but we drive potential and existing customers there.

What do you think is the future of blogging?

Blogging's a relatively new way to connect with your current and potential customers, just like Web sites and e-mail were years ago.

Further, innovations like podcasting and videoblogging have kept it from becoming a predictable medium.

CASE STUDY: JUSTIN PREMICK

I see blogging used increasingly by businesses as a tool to get feedback from customers and to build a customer culture — a community of people joined by their use of or interest in a product or service, a place where they can exchange ideas and suggestions for better using what a company offers. The sort of loyalty to a group that this fosters drives repeat business and reduces attrition, and as traditional advertising and marketing get more costly and less effective, I think you'll see more firms turn to blogging.

AWeber Communications, Inc.
http://www.aweber.com
AWeber Blog: http://www.aweber.com/blog
help@aweber.com

Located in Newtown, Pennsylvania, AWeber Communications develops and manages online opt-in e-mail newsletters, follow-up automation, and e-mail deliverability services for small business customers around the world. Customers access our Web site 24/7 to manage and send their newsletters to recipients who have specifically opted in on their Web site to receive that information.

AWeber's founder, Tom Kulzer, believes very strongly in ethical opt-in e-mail marketing and has developed strong policies and procedures to prevent abuse. With zero tolerance for spam abuse Tom is frequently called upon to speak at industry anti-spam conferences. E-mail deliverability management is a large part of daily operations to ensure that the opt-in newsletters for AWeber's thousands of small businesses around the world are reliably delivered. This is also a frequent topic of conference speeches and telephone conference calls. AWeber's Education team also holds weekly live video Webinar training sessions, teaching the basics of ethical opt-in e-mail marketing.

CASE STUDY: HEADSETOPTIONS

www.headsetoptions.org

Can you describe your introduction to blogging, how you became interested, and how has it impacted you personally?

I started by bookmarking news and articles along with my comments online as a digital diary and never shared it with anyone. In one sense I was using what a Weblog really is and not the blog we know today. Eventually, I joined a progressive community of bloggers from Canada and the U.S. that interested me into starting my blog — this time to share it with everyone interested. Since that time, my blog has evolved into a multi-author site with a focus. Our efforts are now more toward the development of tools for a popular CMS called WordPress.

From a business perspective, how do you think blogging can positively impact communications, sales, and corporate image?

Blogging definitely adds value to your business and it is not limited to users in the computer or technology related industries but practically any industry. My experience has been on both sides of the aisle. On one hand, I run a community not-for-profit site relating to the environment, and on the other, a freelance Web design portal offering business solutions via the Internet. Blogging opens your channel of communication at a much more personal level, which in a conventional business setting is less prevalent. Not to mean that blogging is less professional, but rather a far less formal and open platform encouraging greater user participation.

What is the best advice you can give an individual or business who is considering starting a blog?

Don't wait, start your blog today!

More specifically, for businesses, the aim should be to get the community involved. You'll need to be honest, be regular in posting information, and respect one and all. Also, allow commenting. Your blog is just another Web site if there is no social interaction.

As for individuals, in addition to the above info, always remember that thousands of people will read your blog, one of whom might be your mother, so be kind and polite.

What industry sites and blogs do you read regularly?

CASE STUDY: HEADSETOPTIONS

I read a lot of news and the site I visit the most is BBC News. It's a good example of a semi-social news portal. The part I like is the user interactive feature called "Have Your Say," but they moderate comments, which bothers me a bit. Other than that, the ability to share photos and videos is interesting. Considering that BBC news is read by folks from all over the globe, this makes for a very interesting channel to bring out new and different perspectives. I don't get around to visiting many other sites due to time constraints although I would like to.

What are your favorite blog development tools or applications?

Undoubtedly it's WordPress, which is a personal publishing platform. WP (as it's abbreviated) has evolved into a great content management software. Our freelance services are built around WP and its various plugin applications.

Can you name five tips for successful blogging?

- Try and focus your blog on one subject that will generate repeat and loyal readers.

- Be regular in posting; no one wants to visit a site and find the same post each time!

- Be bold, write to your heart's content, and say as you see it. A little bit of notoriety can be good for your blog.

- Be well-informed, check your facts, and be honest about your posts. If you write a paid-post/sponsored post, say so. Do not mislead your readers.

- Be yourself. Don't fake it.

Can you name five common mistakes in blogging?

Here we go. It's just my opinion, but there are many other ways to screw up your credibility:

- Faking authorship by purchasing content is by far the worst. Remember, many other bloggers might purchase the same article and search bots will confuse

CASE STUDY: HEADSETOPTIONS

your content with that of others and will categorize it as duplicates. This could seriously damage your site's standing among search engines.

- Writing about everything that is popular in the blogosphere but never really adding value to it by means of interpretation or opinion. Remember, if I want conventional news, I would go to a news source like Reuters.

- Not standing behind what you write.

- Not focusing on core expertise and writing about topics you are less familiar with only because it's hot!

- Filling your blog with too much advertisements and paid content. Remember, even Google limits the number of ads per page to three for a reason.

What is the best way to get a new blog promoted?

Word of mouth is by far the most effective but probably the least used method. My personal experience has been by actively participating in discussions among your peers and building a reputation as a serious blogger. Also, I gave out freebies, especially blog-related downloads.

What is the relationship between your Web site and your blogs? How are they interconnected? How does the blog expand upon your Web site?

In a nutshell, my Web site is centered on the blog. I use a popular blogging platform to run my site, so the essence of everything that happens on my site is the blog.

What do you think is the future of blogging?

According to Technorati, the blogosphere doubles every ten months. I have personally noticed a growth in bloggers since the time I started in 1998. Back then the word blog did not exist. If it did, I did not know. Now it's a part of everyday life. Just by observing the demand for blogging tools and services, I feel that it is not a trend; it's here to stay.

CASE STUDY: HEADSETOPTIONS

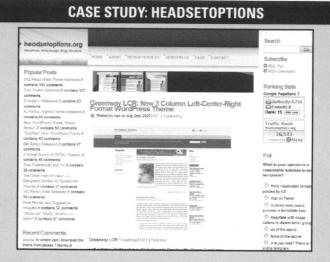

Headsetoptions.org promotes individuals and helps businesses launch, grow, or reinvent themselves by leveraging the power of design to create brand identities and gain market share. Headsetoptions is a highly ranked site by a WordPress enthusiast; the site focuses on all things WordPress. To contact them, e-mail at headsetop@yahoo.com or via **http://www.headsetoptions.org.**

CASE STUDY: JIM DURBIN

www.durbinmedia.com

Can you describe your introduction to blogging, how you became interested, and how has it impacted you personally?

I was reading the Wall Street Journal online in 2001, and they had a link for someone called an Instapundit. I clicked on Glenn's site and was instantly hooked. Blogging personally has made me smarter and more successful. Using blogs, first to discuss politics and my personal life and then later in a business setting, allowed me to look at my life, my business, and my beliefs in a new way. Forced to explain what I believed, I came to understand why I believed as well. In business, blogging transformed me from a second-rate salesperson to a first-rate salesperson and from corporate worker bee to entrepreneur. Using the power of personal branding, I've built a practice as a social media consultant and am now regarded as an expert by colleagues I respect.

From a business perspective, how do you think blogging can positively impact communications, sales, and corporate image?

CASE STUDY: JIM DURBIN

Blogging's biggest and least understood impact is on the bloggers themselves. Writing about your profession and engaging in dialogue with other bloggers and readers sharpens your reading, writing, and critical skills. You research more, debate better, and ultimately make a better employee. For companies who blog, the chance to communicate with an audience through an unfiltered human being supplies the personal touch lacking in most marketing. Done right, it humanizes the corporation. And most important, blogging teaches you skills that allow you to listen to the marketplace. Bloggers don't often suffer from tin ears.

What is the best advice you can give an individual or business who is considering starting a blog?

Read as much as you can from other successful bloggers. Then copy them shamelessly. Make sure you enjoy blogging before you start.

What industry sites and blogs do you read regularly?

Instapundit, Techcrunch, Techdirt, Mashable, web-strategist.com, and about 300 more. I tend to rotate my RSS feeds a lot to keep them fresh.

What are your favorite blog development tools or applications?

Typepad. Personally I believe it is the best tool and better for SEO. The management of the site is easiest with Typepad, and we've run entire sites using Typepad as a content management tool.

Can you name five tips for successful blogging?

Read, have passion, celebrate your audience, comment elsewhere, and learn the etiquette of linking.

Can you name five common mistakes in blogging?

Failing to link to other sites, failure to read critically, getting in blog wars, talking about sex, politics, or religion in a business blog, and being boring.

What is the best way to get a new blog promoted?

CASE STUDY: JIM DURBIN

It's cliché, but it really is best to leave good comments on other industry blogs. If you want to be involved in a community, you have to give something to that community. Reading people regularly and commenting regularly is a good way to start. Unfortunately, most people comment with the express purpose of pitching their new blog, which is not recommended. If you don't have something interesting to say, read more blogs to find a topic where you do have an interest.

What is the relationship between your Web site and your blogs? How are they interconnected? How does the blog expand upon your Web site?

Our blog for the corporate Web site is our main branding tool and drives SEO to our main site. We attached the blog to the main URL for that purpose, and then integrated the blog into the site design. You should always have a link to the blog from your front page, even if it is stand-alone.

What do you think is the future of blogging?

I think blogging is already mainstream, but will be seen as another skill to have, like buying advertising or writing press releases. In five years, every PR department, ad agency, and most marketing departments will have social media experts on staff, and they each will have blogs in their tool belt as a way to connect with a targeted audience. Blogs will grow in importance over podcasts and video for the simple reason that their text is good SEO. As companies realize this, every SEO company will use blogs to increase their search rank.

Jim Durbin is the Director, Corporate Communications for the Durbin Media Group in St. Louis, Missouri. He joined the recruiting world in 1999 at the peak of the Internet bubble in Los Angeles and has since made the transition from staffing account manager to recruiting blogger to social media consultant.

CASE STUDY: JIM DURBIN

He is interested in using the social networking format to improve communication between companies and their customers. His primary blog is for **http://www.brandstorming.com**, a corporate branding and advertising blog he co-authors with his wife, Franki. He also writes at **http://www.stlrecruiting.com**, a local recruiting blog, and **http://www.24thstate.com**, a Missouri political blog.

His interests are social networking, consumer generated media, recruiting, online communities, and the science of social networks. Mr. Durbin is a 1995 graduate of Washington and Lee University. He can be reached at jdurbin@durbinmedia.com or at his Web site, **http://www.durbinmedia.com**.

CASE STUDY: MERYL K. EVANS

www.meryl.net

Can you describe your introduction to blogging, how you became interested, and how has it impacted you personally?

My first blog entry is dated June 1, 2000, before blogging went mainstream. I liked reading Jason Kottke's and Steve Champeon's blogs. In reading their blogs, I learned more about blogging and I always like to try new geeky things. So I registered with Blogger.com and entered my first post.

Originally, I didn't post much or anything meaningful. At the time, most blogs talked about personal lives. Quite honestly, I didn't think anyone cared about my life and I didn't want to come across as a person who likes to talk about herself. My blog evolved and eventually became the more business-like blog it is today.

Blogging keeps my Web site's content fresh to keep the search engines happy with my site. SEO is a big job, something I don't have time to figure out. So I simply post as often as I can, but rarely twice in one day. So many blogs receive constant updates, and I don't think anyone really wants to read my stuff every hour or even every day — so once is enough. I don't think it'd be an effective use of my time to do multiple posts a day. But this doesn't mean no one should do it — it does work for some blogs.

From a business perspective, how do you think blogging can positively impact communications, sales, and corporate image?

CASE STUDY: MERYL K. EVANS

Blogging also lets clients and prospects get to know me and help me gain their trust. I believe bloggers — especially small businesses or one-person businesses — should just share their thoughts and not spend so much time editing. I look back at old posts and catch typos or missing words. It's horrifying, but I let it go; otherwise, I'll waste time obsessing over a single entry.

When I see business blogs that have typos or goofy grammar, I don't hold it against them. The point of the blog is to write it down as you would a journal. I don't edit my paper-based journal entries. Sometimes I'll re-read my entry before I publish it, but I rarely do that. Why? Because I've been working with the entry long enough that I'd have to wait a day to see it with fresh eyes and truly catch all mistakes. The advantage of blogging is instant publishing. Sure, I'll do entries ahead of time, but, again, once I finish an entry — publish.

What is the best advice you can give an individual or business who is considering starting a blog?

Think about why you want to start one. Will it make a difference? Does your target market read blogs? Someone who wants to reach professional home painters may not be a good candidate to start a blog. Think about it — most painters rarely use a computer during the day unless it's for managing transactions. Do they use a computer for business-related information? When they come home after a long day of painting in the heat, do you think they want to get on the computer and think about work?

Also important: Can you keep it updated at least two or three times a week? While some bigwigs can get away with occasional posts, the average person can't. When people see the blog isn't regularly updated, they're most likely not going to come back.

What industry sites and blogs do you read regularly?

Sites and blogs related to writing, marketing, business to business, and technology.

What are your favorite blog development tools or applications?

I use MovableType and WordPress. I am more comfortable with MovableType's backend and tinkering than WordPress. I also use MT on several nonprofit organization sites because it would be easier for the next person who takes over the Webmaster job to use it than WordPress.

CASE STUDY: MERYL K. EVANS

WordPress has a more powerful backend and doesn't waste time with rebuidling. Developers like it better, but from a usability standpoint, it needs help.

Blogger.com is probably the best starting point for anyone who just wants to test the blogging waters.

Can you name five tips for successful blogging?

- Keep the articles short. You're competing with a lot of blogs. If you have a long entry, break it up into two or more entries and you've got your two or three entries for the week.

- Be genuine. Bloggers can sniff out fakes in an instant.

- Make the text readable. This isn't just about the words you use, but also the colors. Gray text on a white background is becoming a nasty trend —gray is harder to read than black. Also, make the default text size large enough since everyone doesn't know how to change the text size through the Web browser.

- Include an about page. This can have information about the site, blog, authors, company, and so on.

- Make it easy for the first time visitor to figure out what your blog is about. When I first named my blog "Meryl's notes," I put it in the navigation menu. One day, I realized that not everyone will know it's a blog and, on top of that, what the blog covers. So I added the tagline, "Things wordy, geeky, and webby" to help readers get an idea of what the content covers.

Can you name five common mistakes in blogging?

- Promoting your site or a blog entry in comments on other blogs.

- Writing blog entries that sound like an ad or PR tool instead of providing honest, valuable information.

- Making it difficult for readers to contact the blogger.

CASE STUDY: MERYL K. EVANS

- Having a big banner (header) on the blog's page. It pushes the content, the most important part, down and below the fold (off the screen). You could lose readers who are just bumming around blogs.

- Playing audio or sound. It freaks people out and it isn't professional in a business blog unless you're in the music business. People expect music pros to have sound. Besides, readers may not share your taste.

What is the best way to get a new blog promoted?

Submit your blogs to RSS and blog directories. This resource lists many of these places: **http://www.masternewmedia.org/rss/top55/**.

Get involved with the blogging community and leave genuine comments.

Many blogs let you include your URL in the comments form — the URL safely promotes your blog.

Write blog entries based on another blog entry you read and link to that blog entry. It shows you read other blogs. Of course, be genuine about it. People know brownnosing when they see it.

Add your blog URL to your e-mail signature. Put it on business cards, flyers, brochures — wherever appropriate. If you write a personal blog, its URL doesn't belong on a business card.

What is the relationship between your Web site and your blogs? How are they interconnected? How does the blog expand upon your Web site?

For some sites, the blog is the site, but not in my case. The blog has played second fiddle to the main part of the site, which explains the services I offer and the benefits. The blog and features (longer entries that resemble full-blown articles) provide the freshest content for my site. The rest of the site doesn't change much and search engines don't like static sites. Since my primary job is writing, the blog and features provide a good way to demonstrate my abilities.

What do you think is the future of blogging?

CASE STUDY: MERYL K. EVANS

Blogging software also makes great content management systems (CMS). I use blogging applications to manage several nonprofit organization Web sites. Knowing that I won't be the Web chair forever, I needed to find a way to make it easy for the next chair to update the site as not all volunteers who step up know much about HTML and Web design.

Like e-mail newsletters and other e-marketing tools, blogs will continue to have a role in marketing. I believe the number of new blogs will reach a tipping point when everyone knows what they are and what they can do.

Some businesses have discovered that a blog doesn't work for them. Those using blogs on a personal basis will tire of updating the blog and new bloggers will step in and take their place preventing the numbers from going up. The cycle repeats.

People thought e-mail newsletters would go away because of spam, feeds, and blogs. But they're still one of the best returns on investment for businesses. Blogs will face the same thing. People might think they'll go away because there are too many of them and only so much time in the day to read them. But they will have value whether it's as a CMS, relationship builder, or a place to share your life with the world out there.

The most important thing to remember when blogging: If you interview for a new job, do you want the interviewee or manager to see what you wrote in your blog? It's very common for human resources and managers to search for a candidate's info on the Internet.

Meryl K. Evans, Content Maven behind meryl.net, has written and edited for AbsoluteWrite, ECT News Network, The Dallas Morning News, Digital Web, Lockergnome, MarketingProfs, PC Today, O'Reilly, Pearson, Sams, Wiley, and WROX.

CASE STUDY: MERYL K. EVANS

She has written copy for businesses as well as Fib-or-Not? and Meet, Mix, and Mingle games.

Meryl writes and edits content for businesses and publications. She helps business build and maintain relationships with clients and prospects.

She is Editor-in-Chief of Shavlik's The Remediator Security Digest, a popular newsletter on computer security with over 100,000 subscribers.

She's also the editor of Professional Service Journal, an e-mail newsletter for business-to-business service providers, Intel Solution Services' Connected Digest, and TailoredMail's Focus eJournal. Meryl's the author of Brilliant Outlook Pocketbooks.

Meryl is an educator with New York University's online graduate program.

She has worked for two Fortune 500 telecom companies, the U.S. federal government in Washington, D.C. and IT consulting. A native Texan, she lives a heartbeat north of Dallas in Plano, Texas with her husband and three kiddos.

CASE STUDY: SMORTY.COM

Can you describe your introduction to blogging, how you became interested, and how has it impacted you personally?

Smorty is a blog advertising company. We focus on building a network of the highest quality blogs rather than a large network of poor quality blogs. This brings our advertisers a better result for their search engine rankings and traffic — in other words, a better result for their money.

From a business perspective, how do you think blogging can positively impact communications, sales, and corporate image?

Blog advertising is a natural way to build a brand and exposure on the Internet. By having random people writing their positive perspective of your services it reflects on your business brand and builds higher search engine rankings for your keywords.

CASE STUDY: SMORTY.COM

The higher the exposure and the higher your rankings, the more traffic from interested visitors you will receive.

What is the best advice you can give an individual or business who is considering starting a blog?

Write about something you love. Don't waste your time writing about something you may think others will like. You will only become bored and your readers will notice.

What industry sites and blogs do you read regularly?

I read about how blogs are making money.

What are your favorite blog development tools or applications?

Smorty actually runs a blog optimization page on our Web site: **http://www.smorty. com/g/9358/blog-optimization.html.**

Can you name five tips for successful blogging?

Write about something you love, use keywords throughout all your posts, write short sentences so people can understand what you write, don't only write paid advertisements, and get good software when you start your blog, not after.

Can you name five common mistakes in blogging?

Lack of research, poor writing skills, no common topic, too many ads, and bad software choice.

What is the best way to get a new blog promoted?

Use **http://www.smorty.com/g/9358/blog-optimization.html** and Feedburner and build inbound links.

Smorty is a blog advertising company. You can find them online at **www.smorty. com.**

CASE STUDY: PAUL STAMATIOU

http://paulstamatiou.com

Can you describe your introduction to blogging, how you became interested, and how has it impacted you personally?

My fascination with blogging began in 2005 as a curiosity for various pieces of software that facilitate blogging. I started out installing WordPress locally on my Mac and began tinkering with developing themes. One day I ended up buying PaulStamatiou.com, got a Web hosting account, and went live. Two years later I realized how powerful a blog can be and how people have come to enjoy my writing. I feel that my blog is a résumé for me, as I am still in college, so I keep everything on it as professional as possible.

From a business perspective, how do you think blogging can positively impact communications, sales, and corporate image?

In the last few years, business blogs have become more and more popular. Companies have started branching out from their predominantly press release media outreach ways and embraced the blog way of reaching out to their customers, users, supporters, and followers. I learned a lot about the background behind business blogs when I helped Yahoo! develop and launch their corporate blog, Yodel Anecdotal, as an intern last summer. Business blogs can put a face on the company, so to speak, and cast a favorable, friendly light on an otherwise bland corporate image.

What is the best advice you can give an individual or business who is considering starting a blog?

Just do it! If I never stirred up the curiosity to start my blog, I would not have grown a loyal readership that I now know personally and communicate with at a moment's notice. My only advice is that, if you plan on starting a blog, you need to devote time to update it. There is nothing worse than an outdated blog.

What industry sites and blogs do you read regularly?

Since I write about technology and am generally interested by things of that subject matter, I subscribe to the big dogs in the tech field: Engadget, The Unofficial Apple Weblog, Ars Technica, AnandTech, Uneasy Silence, Digg, O'Reilly Radar, TechMeme, and Wired.

CASE STUDY: PAUL STAMATIOU

What are your favorite blog development tools or applications?

When it comes to doing anything on a computer, my operating system of choice is Apple's OS X. It's a personal choice, but I just find the interface more intuitive to use and there happen to be a lot more developer-friendly tools for OS X. I rely on the Firebug add-on for the Firefox browser for debugging my blog's theme, Photoshop CS3 for making any graphics for my blog, Transmit for everything FTP-related, and TextMate for editing and writing code. It also helps my development workflow now that I have a 30-inch LCD display.

Can you name five tips for successful blogging?

- Maintain a steady posting schedule. If you're going to blog every two days, keep it like that. Your readers won't think much of you if you don't post for eight days.

- Get to know people who maintain similar blogs.

- Comment on different blogs frequently. That will get your name out there and increase your blog's exposure over time.

- Make it easy for people to subscribe to your blog by having an RSS feed or subscription via e-mail module visible on your blog. Feedburner is a great place to look for both of these things.

- Choose a topic and stick with it. You are much more likely to find an audience for a blog centered around technology than you are if you randomly post about different topics every day.

Can you name five common mistakes in blogging?

- Forgetting about your blog and not updating it frequently.

- Not replying to comments posted on your blog. If someone takes the time to comment on one of your articles, you should acknowledge their comment, reply to their question if they have one, and the like. It lets them know that there is actually someone taking care of the site and reading their comments. This also helps to establish a rapport with your readers.

CASE STUDY: PAUL STAMATIOU

- Having a slow blog. Don't clutter your blog with slow-loading widgets, large images, or other superfluous items. A usability study recently showed that if your site does not completely load within four seconds, most people will leave.

- Maintaining a non-professional blog. What I mean to say is, you will attract a wider audience if your blog is clean of bad words and spam comments. While some blogs can get away with expletives, as that's how they relate to their specific audience, it's just better to play it safe and family friendly.

- "Selling out" is one way to lose your readers' trust. Currently, many paid review services have been sprouting up. With these services, the blogger gets paid to review a product on their blog. From personal experiences with these services I have learned through my readers that they don't appreciate those type of posts, even if I write them in what I believed was an unbiased stance. As a blogger once said, "A paid review is a biased review."

What is the best way to get a new blog promoted?

The easiest way to promote a blog is to tell all your friends and comment on many similar blogs. The best way to promote a blog is to get it featured on a popular social news and bookmarking site, like Digg or del.icio.us. Achieving something like that is by far no small feat but results in massive initial traffic and picking up some new subscribers. Another way is to contact authors of popular blogs that talk about similar topics and let them know about your new site. Chances are they won't write about you immediately if at all, but people love finding out about new sites and they might become subscribers themselves. Also, it is better to write a few articles before actively promoting your site. If you promote it when it only has one post on it, people will glance over it and leave.

What is the relationship between your Web site and your blogs? How are they interconnected? How does the blog expand upon your Web site?

For me, my blog is a Web site in itself. It has static pages like regular Web sites, in addition to the frequently updated blog section. It's just one big seamless Web site with the blog taking center stage.

What do you think is the future of blogging?

CASE STUDY: PAUL STAMATIOU

With the future of blogging, blogs will be more thoroughly embraced by everyone from teens to massive corporations. Companies like Yahoo! and General Motors maintain top-notch corporate blogs that are setting an example for others to follow. Blogs are a great way to find others online with the same interests as you and they provide a place for interaction to occur. In the future, blogging software will be amazingly easy-to-use, update, and run by yourself. These technical barriers have been allayed with the development of hosted blogging solutions like **WordPress.com** and **Blogger.com**, but there is always room for improvement.

Paul Stamatiou is a 21-year-old Computational Media student at the Georgia Institute of Technology. He has been blogging for two years on his technology blog, PaulStamatiou.com. His blog receives over 200,000 page views per month and has 5,000 subscribers. Paul was also an intern for Yahoo!, where he helped roll out their corporate blog at **yodel.yahoo.com.**

CASE STUDY: GREGORY A. WHITE

http://www.tbredtech.com

Can you describe your introduction to blogging, how you became interested, and how has it impacted you personally?

I was looking for a methodology to use to simplify the process of keeping a site fresh. At the same time I was also looking for a way to do journaling on the Web. Blogs satisfied both those needs.

From a business perspective, how do you think blogging can positively impact communications, sales, and corporate image?

They can significantly increase each.

What is the best advice you can give an individual or business who is considering starting a blog?

- If you have your own Web site, then select a blog application on which there is good support and a good aftermarket. I use WordPress.

- If you don't have your own Web site use **http://blogger.com.**

CASE STUDY: GREGORY A. WHITE

- Set your blog up, write a couple of articles, submit them to **ezinearticles.com**, and use a link in your resource box to point back to your blog.

- Post at least once a week.

What industry sites and blogs do you read regularly?

- Guy Kawasaki's "How To Change The World"

- Seth Godin's Blog

What are your favorite blog development tools or applications?

- WordPress (WordPress Plugins)

- **http://www.top200-blog-rss-submit.com**

- **http://tagplusbookmarks.com**

- **http://www.web2me2.com**

- **http://www.web2me2.com/bookmark/index.php?url=http://socialbuzzmaster.com&title=Social+Buzz+Master+Pre-Launch**

- **http://socialbuzzmaster.com**

Can you name five tips for successful blogging?

- Visit lots of top blogs in your industry and leave real comments.

- Post at least once a week and where you're able use quotes from top blogs using trackback. That way your post will appear not only on your page but a reference link will appear on their page.

- Use a button from **http://www.web2me2.com/bookmark** at the bottom of your post.

CASE STUDY: GREGORY A. WHITE

- Promote each post using Social Bookmarking.

- Submit your blog and RSS feeds to all the blog and RSS feed directories and ping your blog after every post.

Can you name five common mistakes in blogging?

- Expecting your blog to do the marketing without marketing your blog. Blogs are a great marketing tool but need to be marketed themselves. People often want to use the blog to do the marketing of other sites and fail to market the blog.

- Not posting often enough. Give your readers something to look forward to. Leave them hanging.

- Not using RSS Feed Chicklets. Give your readers a chance to subscribe to your feed.

- Not using Social Bookmarking. Give your readers a chance to bookmark interesting posts.

- Not using a subscription form to get subscribers.

What is the best way to get a new blog promoted?

- Create articles and submit them to http://ezinearticles.com.

- Short-Term Tactic — Social Bookmarking and Social News Sites

- Long-Term Tactic — RSS feeds to feed directories and blog to blog directories

- Additionally submit blogs to online directories

What is the relationship between your Web site and your blogs? How are they interconnected? How does the blog expand upon your Web site?

CASE STUDY: GREGORY A. WHITE

- Just about every Web site I have has a blog.

- Some blogs are News Blogs, providing up-to-the-minute news on specific topics:

  o Web 2.0

  o Viral Videos

  o Social Bookmarking

  o RC Car Meets

  o Paintball Competitions

- Some are Tip Blogs that provide tips on certain topics:

  o Traffic Generation Tips

  o Paintball Strategies

- Some are Data Feed Blogs (online stores):

  o General Nutrition products

  o Jewelry

- Some blogs are Corporate Blogs providing image and information

Blogs provide a rich source of current information that make a site come alive.

What do you think is the future of blogging?

- Its future is vibrant

- I just believe blogging has a great future.

Greg White is a full-time project manager and software developer for a commercial software development company that makes a File Tracking System and a Loan Records Tracking System.

He has been developing Web projects since 1998 for companies like Shell Oil, Texaco, and organizations like the University of Houston and has been marketing on the Internet since about 2001. He has also been doing software development since 1981.

CASE STUDY: GREGORY A. WHITE

Greg White, PMP, MCSD, MCDBA, MCSE, MCT
Project Manager
Thoroughbred Technologies, Inc.
10701 Corporate Drive, Suite 288
gawhite@tbredtech.com
greg_white@earthlink.net
http://www.tbredtech.com
281-491-6787 Ext. 231 direct | 832-654-7441 mobile
281-491-6776 fax

Greg has provided the following resources for bloggers who want to get the word out about their topics:

- **http://www.top200-blog-rss-submit.com**

- **http://top200-blog-rss-submit.com/dl/index.htm**

- **http://tagplusbookmarks.com**

- **http://www.tagplusbookmarks.com/tpdl/cb_tpsblthankyou.htm**

- **http://www.web2me2.com (Beta)**

- **http://www.web2me2.com/bookmark — to set up a button**

- **http://www.web2me2.com/bookmark/index.php?url=http:// socialbuzzmaster.com&title=Social+Buzz+Master+Pre-Launch (site in use)**

- **http://socialbuzzmaster.com — in pre-launch**

- **http://discount-plr-monthly.com — for inexpensive private label rights content.**

CASE STUDY: JACK HUMPHREY

http://www.fridaytrafficreport.com
http://www.authoritysitecenter.com

Can you describe your introduction to blogging, how you became interested, and how has it impacted you personally?

As a professional Internet marketer I became interested in blogs as a way to expand our business and hit new markets when the first blogs began to report success in being able to generate real leads and profits in niche industries.

At one point it was taboo to make money or generate leads with a blogging platform. For some hold outs in the blogging world, it is still a matter of poor taste. Because of the mistaken belief that blogs were just for public diaries and nothing more, marketers couldn't see the opportunity they presented to their businesses and didn't know how to use them to generate interest in their products and services.

Early in 2005 we began to see that certain bloggers were generating massive publicity with their free content and that blogging was growing up to include serious topics in many niches that were attracting strong readership. This translated into business for the bloggers as relationships were built with their readers.

We succeeded in our early market tests and since created an entire business out of showing marketers how they could attract real customers through blogging with high quality content. From a technology standpoint, blogs are now some of the most advanced content management systems available, offering marketers far more control and marketing capabilities than static sites.

If commercialized or "sponsored" blogging had not become accepted by Internet users, we'd be in a different business today. And our business would not have the ability it has through blogging to generate tens of thousands of leads per month to push our own products and affiliated products and services our market is looking for.

From a business perspective, how do you think blogging can positively impact communications, sales, and corporate image?

Because surfers trust blogs that have an obvious slant toward providing high quality content on a regular basis, they don't care if those blogs are monetized through

CASE STUDY: JACK HUMPHREY

sponsorships, pay-per-click advertising, and links to the blog owner's products or services as long as the ads are not overbearing.

If you understand giving away very significant and valuable content in order to attract the kind of loyalty and brand recognition only blogging can give you, you can generate high search engine rankings and hundreds or thousands of links from sites related to your niche that drive targeted, eager prospects right to your doorstep.

What is the best advice you can give an individual or business who is considering starting a blog?

My best advice for an individual or business who is considering starting a blog is to use WordPress. From our extensive testing of various blog platforms, WordPress is the most optimized out of the box and can be tweaked for much tighter search engine optimization with myriad plugins.

Since WordPress is "pen source and is the most widely used self-hosted blogging platform on the Web, with over one million downloads, anyone can develop plugins for it and many programmers do. More so than any other blog system on the Web.

There is more support available for WordPress because it has a large user community and it is easier to find independent techs who know WordPress and who can help businesses tweak it for their specific needs.

Since WordPress is the household name in blogging, there are also far more people who provide advanced training and marketing tactics directly related to WordPress and a wide variety of plugins that make it a very powerful publishing system in the right hands.

What industry sites and blogs do you read regularly?

Copyblogger.com, Problogger.net, SearchEngineLand.com, **http://www.seomoz. org/blog, SEOBook.com**, Seth Godin's blog at **http://sethgodin.typepad.com/seths_ blog/, Technorati.com, http://googleblog.blogspot.com/,** Matt Cutts at **http://www. mattcutts.com/blog/.**

What are your favorite blog development tools or applications?

WordPress, **MyBlogLog.com, Technorati.com, FeedBurner.com, FeedBlitz.com.**

CASE STUDY: JACK HUMPHREY

Can you name five tips for successful blogging?

- Very regular content development and posting. Readers hate to see a stagnant blog and the engines very quickly learn when a blog isn't updated regularly and stop rewarding those blogs with rankings.

- Write remarkable original content that the reader will not only bookmark and use again and again, but tell others about on their blogs and via e-mail.

- Use social marketing and Web 2.0 sites to post your content in order to drive targeted traffic and authoritative links to your site on a regular basis.

- Know your keywords and what you most need to show up in the search engines and write a lot of content around those topics.

- Use e-mail capture like FeedBlitz.com to allow readers to subscribe to your RSS feed via e-mail and put your RSS subscription methods in plain sight for all your visitors to see. This will drastically increase your return visitor ratio in the long run.

Can you name five common mistakes in blogging?

- Letting a blog go static. People make mental notes when surfing and finding a blog that has not been updated. And you only have one chance to impress a first time visitor.

- Not capturing e-mails for follow-up.

- Reprinting too much third party content.

- Not learning the language of the blogosphere. Making very long, technical, dry posts is a big no no. You can cover most any topic with a blog, but remember that you are competing with other interesting and entertaining blogs. Do something to make your information pithy, targeted, to the point, and entertaining. Link to a PDF with full text on a longer piece and give a summary or teaser in your post to avoid click-offs.

- Not working daily to get your content pushed out to Web 2.0 news sites and not taking enough time to understand the blogosphere and how it really works to gain attention, links, and traffic.

CASE STUDY: JACK HUMPHREY

What is the best way to get a new Weblog promoted?

Web 2.0 news sites, for authoritative links and almost immediate traffic and recognition by the search engines. Not posting blog content to places like Digg.com, Netscape.com, and StumbleUpon.com is one of the biggest mistakes new bloggers make.

What is the relationship between your Web site and your blogs? How are they interconnected? How does the blog expand upon your Web site?

My blog is the face of my company. It is where the rubber meets the road. Our various product Web sites depend almost completely on the traffic gathered by our blogs. Since static Web sites have fallen out of favor with the engines, our blogs are the major factor determining whether we get enough leads to thrive and sell our products.

What do you think is the future of blogging?

Blogging will continue to become the mainstream Internet publishing and lead generation platform. It will eventually be seen as something more than blogging and be accepted as a business publishing platform unto itself.

More and more tools are being developed by companies like ours to make blogging systems more high-powered marketing systems. Even today it is hard to find a successful business on the Web that does not utilize blogging in their marketing and outreach. In the future more and more companies will understand that blogging is an important way to drive traffic and that building a Web presence without a blogging platform and content development plan is a big mistake.

In the future it will become harder and harder to recognize what we do as blogging. To us, it is a search engine optimization system, a customer acquisition and retention system, a product fulfillment system, and a link magnet.

Jack is a marketing consultant and professional speaker who has been marketing on the Web for the past ten years.

He is the owner and editor of The Friday Traffic Report at **http://www.fridaytrafficreport. com.** He is also the CEO of Authority Site Center at **http://www.authoritysitecenter. com** and the author of Power Linking 5th Edition **http://www.power-linking-profits. com** and the Authority Black Book **http://www.authorityblackbook.com.**

CASE STUDY: JACK HUMPHREY

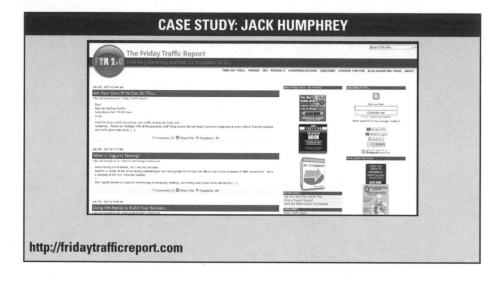

http://fridaytrafficreport.com

CASE STUDY: PATSI KRAKOFF & DENISE WAKEMAN

www.blogsquad.biz

The Blog Squad

Can you describe your introduction to blogging, how you became interested, and how has it impacted you personally?

In 2004 I got an e-mail from Debbie Weil repeating her claim that blogs were a good business marketing tool, and for some reason I took action that day.

It was September 4, 2004, my birthday; because I had a shoulder injury I couldn't play tennis (my other job), I sat down to see if I could set up a blog with Typepad in under an hour.

Not being technologically trained or inclined, I wasn't sure I could do this; but I did.

The lights went on: I had a way to self-publish content on the Web and be in control of how it looked. I e-mailed my partner, Denise Wakeman, and she set up a blog, too. We immediately saw the possibilities for the clients we worked with who wanted to have a strong Web presence and didn't have tech skills or big budgets.

We weren't prepared for what happened next. Initially I was using my blog to publish content for an ebook on how to publish an electronic newsletter. After three,

CASE STUDY: PATSI KRAKOFF & DENISE WAKEMAN

months content for an ebook on how to publish an electronic newsletter. After three months, traffic to my static Web site doubled; in three more months it tripled. Clients started finding me and revenues doubled in a short time. The only thing I was doing differently was blogging two to three times a week.

When I started blogging daily, traffic to the blog doubled.

Personally, I have been amazed at the responsiveness of readers who comment, who are interested in what we say and do, and who have also become joint venture partners. It's the smartest marketing tool I've ever used and it only costs a bit of time: under an hour a day.

My partner and I incorporated and became the Blog Squad, with a mission to help other professionals and small businesses learn how to harness the marketing power of blogs. We wrote the manual on how to set up a blog and optimize it for business: www.buildabetterblogsystem.com.

From a business perspective, how do you think blogging can positively impact communications, sales, and corporate image?

It is a powerful communications tool in many ways. First, you can talk to your ideal readers, clients, and prospects in an informal way. When an individual in the company blogs about what is going on, how to use products and services, problems and solutions, etc., it opens the doors to authentic customer service.

Blogs are interactive and allow a dialogue between the customer and the blog author (could be the CEO or another person). But it is essential that all company jargon and corporate-speak be avoided in favor of having a conversation. Use the first person and sign your name, so readers know who is writing the blog post.

Write with the reader's needs in mind, and you can't go wrong. Be authentic and honest. Allow criticisms and negative comments and always respond respectfully.

You are building relationships with readers, not selling to them. The more you can connect on a human level the better. You can do this without being too personal or revealing details of your life. Do not misuse a business blog or use it as a diary.

Case in point:

CASE STUDY: PATSI KRAKOFF & DENISE WAKEMAN

We love to hear business blog success stories and yesterday we received one from a client we set up a blog for last April. Mark Siegel of Golfasian.com sent us an update on how his blog, Thailand Golf Zone, has impacted his business in the last year. If you're not convinced of the value of adding a business blog to your marketing mix, you must read this unsolicited testimonial.

"My blog now has over 200 posts, all original content, and it has been the single best action I have taken in the way of marketing for my company and myself. I estimate that traffic has increased to my site by 50 percent and have seen over $250,000 of new business come in just from people reading the blog and gaining confidence in dealing with my Thailand golf travel company. Please feel free to use me as a reference or referral for any small business owners who are looking to greatly improve their profile and reputation with their clients. Thank you for your help with the initial set up and all of your great suggestions."

Mark Siegel, Managing Director
Golfasian.com Co. Ltd.
+66-(0)2-714-9770
http://www.golfasian.com and **http://www.thailandgolfzone.com**
The golf experts in Thailand!

Another example:

Bud Bilanich is The Common Sense Guy. He was also one of The Blog Squad's early blogging clients. It was some time in 2005 that we set up Bud's blog, www. CommonSenseGuy.com, on TypePad.com. Bud took to blogging like you wouldn't believe.

Yesterday Bud Bilanich sent us a copy of a chapter he is contributing to a book called One Great Idea. His great idea is that he decided to use a blog to brand himself and his business. And he credits The Blog Squad for teaching him everything he knows about blogging.

For more case studies visit: **http://www.buildabetterblog.com/testimonials/index. html**.

What is the best advice you can give an individual or business who is considering starting a blog?

CASE STUDY: PATSI KRAKOFF & DENISE WAKEMAN

Before jumping in, research other blogs in your field, especially your competitors'. Find out what others are doing and start reading and commenting on blogs you like with meaningful contributions.

When you do launch your blog you will already be known in the blogosphere and people will come visit your blog.

Then clarify your goals: Who are your ideal readers? What is the goal for your blog? How will you launch and drive initial traffic? Make it easy for readers to subscribe, with both RSS feeds and by e-mail. Be sure to put a descriptive tag line in the banner and include your name as blog author.

Find out what most common business blog mistakes are and don't make those errors. We have plenty of free information on our blog, or do a search.

Submit your blog to blog directories. Post a minimum two to three times a week. Keep at it. It may take a while to reach a critical mass of readers before you start to get comments. Always ask readers to comment. Don't give up. Follow your traffic stats and find out what gets results. Don't ignore keyword information and use them in titles and posts.

What industry sites and blogs do you read regularly?

I regularly track blogs about writing for my writing blog, blogs about copywriting, and quite a few on Internet marketing and business blogging. Since we have ten blogs between the two of us, most of them are focused on one of those three niches: writing for the web, blogging, and Internet marketing.

www.copyblogger.com, www.blogwriteforCEOs.com, and **www.webinknow.com** are favorites.

What are your favorite blog development tools or applications?

Typepad is our favorite because of its ease of use for non-tech people. Most professionals don't want to spend their time learning about blog tools and applications; Typepad upgrades their system all the time and offers good e-mail support. Professionals can spend their time writing good content that will bring them good traffic and business instead of messing with the inner workings.

CASE STUDY: PATSI KRAKOFF & DENISE WAKEMAN

Since blogging, I've learned more about how they work and we now offer set-up services with WordPress. But Typepad is still our favorite.

As far as widgets and applications and tools go, we also highly recommend Feedblitz for e-mail subscription services and SiteMeter for tracking traffic.

Can you name five tips for successful blogging?

- Write frequently using keywords in your field. You don't have to learn search engine optimization strategies to be smart about this. How do people look for you or your services on the Web? Are you using those common keyword phrases in different ways in your titles and posts?

- Write frequently using short paragraphs and get to the point. Don't waste readers' time with too much personal info. On the other hand, share some details with them to show you're a human being just like they are.

- Link to other bloggers, Web sites, books, etc., and always cite your sources of information.

- Don't just share information you find — include your personal opinion or perspective. Don't be afraid to disagree, but always be respectful. Ask your readers what they think.

- Write frequently on other blogs by leaving meaningful contributions without self-referencing.

In summary: Write frequently! Just make sure it has value to your targeted readers. And don't forget to ask readers to do something every time: Respond, comment, think, go register, go buy. You're not blogging for your ego; you're blogging for business.

Can you name five common mistakes in blogging?

- Can you believe that many otherwise smart business professionals forget to put their name in their blog banner or tag line? Make sure your name is up top on your blog.

- Can you believe some smart bloggers don't make the link to their Web site

CASE STUDY: PATSI KRAKOFF & DENISE WAKEMAN

obvious? They don't link to their products and services and don't make it clear how people can hire them or buy from them.

- And they also forget to put an e-mail subscription form on their blog — or they bury it down at the bottom. Most people still don't know how to use RSS feeds and prefer to get e-mailed updates to your blog posts. Make it easy for them.

- Stay on target. Because blogs were originally used as online diaries, they still have that reputation. While they should be more informal and conversational, please, your blog is a business blog and nobody really cares about what you do or experience unless there is something in it for them. Always write with the reader in mind.

- Many bloggers forget to ask readers to comment. Or they'll post important information without sharing their personal perspective or opinion. You can't expect readers to comment and share their thoughts unless you do so first. Share and then ask them to share their thoughts.

What is the best way to get a new blog promoted?

Through other people. You can do a lot to invite people on your list to visit your blog and subscribe, and you must do all that you can do. But the real key to growing your blog readership is through other blogs and other people's lists. You can't do that by asking them; you must first build a relationship. Then, make it attractive to them by offering something for free. Starting a contest or a survey with a free prize is a great way to promote your blog. Get viral, create buzz, and use every relationship you can. Other ways include announcing it in your newsletter and posting an online press release.

What is the relationship between your Web site and your blogs? How are they interconnected? How does the blog expand upon your Web site?

Some people worry about whether to host their blog on their Web site or have it free standing on a third-party provider like Typepad. We say it doesn't matter. If it is free standing, you will get lots of traffic to your blog. You will, of course, link over to your Web site and some of the blog visitors will go there, but the fact is this:

You are your own blog author and therefore you are getting the traffic. Does it matter if it is to your blog or to your Web site? Not really. We say follow this:

CASE STUDY: PATSI KRAKOFF & DENISE WAKEMAN

- Get published

- Get found

- Get leads

Then what you do with those leads is another story and another part of your marketing plan. Blogs can do these first three tasks well. But that's a start and not the finish.

Blogging is a communications tool that we use to build credibility and trust. Since readers aren't going to hire us based on a static brochure-type Web site, our blog acts as a way for prospects to get to know us and like us.

What do you think is the future of blogging?

I love this question and I've answered it many times since 2004 in the same way:

In five years nobody will be talking about blogs because all Web sites will be built on blogging platforms.

I haven't changed my answer. The thing is, it will not take five years. It is happening already. There are many Web sites today that are created with blog software.

In the end, it doesn't matter. What matters most is this: Is your Web presence working for you to grow your business?

Do you have a way to get published, get found, and get leads? Can clients, readers, and prospects easily find you, get to know you, and interact with you and your company?

Right now, having a blog set up for business purposes and writing on it frequently is the best bang for your marketing buck.

Blog on!

Patsi Krakoff and Denise Wakeman are The Blog Squad™ and have teamed up to help professionals and small businesses harness the power of blogs, newsletters, and ecommerce systems to make marketing tasks easier and attract, sell, and profit. Between them, they have 18 years of Interent know-how and write on ten blogs.

CASE STUDY: PATSI KRAKOFF & DENISE WAKEMAN

They know what works! You can read their popular blog at **www.BuildaBetterBlog.com** and get their free weekly e-zine Savvy eBiz Tips at **www.SavvyeBizTips.com** .

Internet marketing confusing? ... Wondering how you can be found on the web by your prospects?

If you're a speaker, author or service professional, you know how important it is to be "findable" on the Web to grow your business and get more clients.

And, here's what else you need to know:

SAVVY EBIZ TIPS

Savvy eBiz Tips | Weekly Blog-Zine
Savvy eBiz Tips RSS Feed

GET TO KNOW THE BLOG SQUAD

Marketing on The Web
Free Resources to Help Your Business Grow

www.theblogsquad.biz

CASE STUDY: JENS MEIERT

www.meiert.com/en/

Can you describe your introduction to blogging, how you became interested, and how has it impacted you personally?

Well, there are two stories. In 2003 I started to regularly publish my German Web development and usability articles and translations on my Web site (meiert.com), and some people consider that German site a blog even though it doesn't even allow comments. (I don't think that comment functionality is necessary for a blog, but it appears to be characteristic.) In 2005 I thought about establishing an English blog (meiert.com/en), which finally went live in January 2007. This real blog was driven by the wish to contribute to a more global audience, as well as just talking about things that bother or please me and other professionals.

Personally, I enjoy blogs because of the close proximity between authors and readers — blogs bring people together. Feeds and comments make it easy to get and stay informed and involved, and I appreciate that both from an author's and a reader's

CASE STUDY: JENS MEIERT

point of view. The impact blogging has on me is best described by two aspects: more responsibility and higher involvement.

From a business perspective, how do you think blogging can positively impact communications, sales, and corporate image?

To be honest, I still consider corporate blogging a double-edged sword. On the one hand, it's basically a great thing in order to build more trust and credibility, which will result in more sales and better reputation. On the other hand, this only works when those corporate bloggers can really be sincere and when there is no corporate censorship involved. (At least, they need to convey that impression all the time.)

The problem is that this is just not possible in every company; I very much doubt that. Especially larger companies will have a higher probability of either letting people blog who are not quite happy about certain things — at first, this is probably perceived positively since credible, but from a certain point on it will backfire — choosing only certain people — that's also censorship — or establishing any kind of blog supervision.

From a corporate perspective, you just need to make sure that nobody can question your truthfulness. As an outsider, you can only hope for that honesty or probably become at least a little bit paranoid.

What is the best advice you can give an individual or business who is considering starting a blog?

Be sincere and focus on accurateness; focus on quality.

What industry sites and blogs do you read regularly?

That's quite a bunch. I'll randomly pick five:

* Kaiser Fung, **http://junkcharts.typepad.com/**

* InfoDesign, **http://www.informationdesign.org/**

* Donald Norman, **http://www.jnd.org/**

* SEOmoz, **http://www.seomoz.org/blog**

* Anne van Kesteren, **http://annevankesteren.nl/**

CASE STUDY: JENS MEIERT

What are your favorite blog development tools or applications?

I definitely appreciate and recommend WordPress. Other blog systems — I evaluated quite a few before setting up English meiert.com — are almost always less usable, less maintainable, or output worse code. However, I won't recommend any development tools, plugins (except for Akismet, which does a great job in filtering spam), and stuff, since this is just too individual. The needs are too different.

Can you name five tips for successful blogging?

- Write accurate content

- Write regularly

- Be social

- Be honest

- Be passionate

Can you name five common mistakes in blogging?

Provocatively yet wisely, there's only one mistake:

- Not learning from mistakes

What is the best way to get a new blog promoted?

Unless it's just for fun, you're better off setting goals for your blog first, whatever they are. It makes it easier to strike.

Configure your blog to ping Technorati, Google Blog Search, and pals. Create a few posts that are well-researched, comprehensive, and/or provocative, but in a way that's roughly similar to the style you will adhere to in the near future. Tell your friends and colleagues; some of them might even want to link to your blog. Make use of trustworthy and relevant blog and feed directories. Use opportunities to get links to your blog; for example, in public profiles of LinkedIn and stuff. Learn and optimize. (That never ends, unfortunately. Or fortunately.)

What is the relationship between your Web site and your blogs? How are they interconnected? How does the blog expand upon your Web site?

CASE STUDY: JENS MEIERT

Well, on the one hand, my blog is relatively closely linked to its German sister due to the same corporate identity, some shared content that is just available in two languages, and some architectural commonalities. On the other hand, it's quite different: It targets a different — the English — information space with often different material. It is based on dynamic pages, whereas the rest of the site is still static.

However, this hybrid concept seems to work pretty well, even though English readers can hardly benefit from the German part of my site. (It is actually even more professional, covering all my professional publications, from books to articles to translations.)

What do you think is the future of blogging?

Blog software will anticipate posts and hammer them out to all social networking platforms available.

Seriously: For the near future, I expect greater simplification and more automation. (Quite abstract, sure.) I also expect more information space pollution, meaning relatively less posts containing new and valuable information, and much more spam, meaning more than 20 spam comments for one real comment. I don't expect anything revolutionary, though: This would require new names or buzzwords, respectively, and will not be called blogging.

Jens Meiert is a Web Design Specialist and Artist from Bremen, Germany.

Beside his engagement for W3C (formerly WCAG, currently HTML Working Group), UPA, and IxDA, he's also author of several articles and books (Webdesign mit CSS, O'Reilly), as well as the man behind the The World's Highest Website. You'll find more details about Jens Meiert and his work on his Web site, **http://www.meiert.com/en/.**

http://www.meiert.com/en/

CASE STUDY: JOHN PAUL MICEK

http://www.TribalSeduction.com
http://www.AdvancedBusinessBlogging.com
www.RPMsuccess.com

Can you describe your introduction to blogging, how you became interested, and how has it impacted you personally?

In 2001 I sold two of my businesses in New Jersey and we moved to Hawaii to start a new business where we would work with entrepreneurs from around the world.

When we decided to run our international coaching and consulting business from the middle of the Pacific, our family and friends thought we were nuts. We struggled at first trying to get traditional forms of Internet marketing to work, but none had the level of influence and rapport-building power we were looking for.

Then a little over three years ago we started to get involved with new media like blogs, podcasts, and social networks. That has been a much better match to our style of sales and marketing. The results have been nothing short of spectacular.

On the SEO side, we have used specially optimized blogs to get and keep top search engine rankings, page ranks of five and higher, thousands of inbound links, and tens of thousands of visitors to our sites each month.

And more importantly we've done it all online achieving real bottom line business building results like:

- Acquire over $700,000 in private consultation contracts with dozens of Fortune 500 companies, including Monsanto, New England Financial, Solomon Smith Barney, Coldwell Banker, and more

- Work with three of the top five largest corporations in Hawaii (all initiated online)

- Coach, advise, and strategize with leading politicians in states across the U.S.

- Personally invited to speak to thousands of business people from Australia to Detroit, Singapore to New York City, and everywhere in between by

CASE STUDY: JOHN PAUL MICEK

professional organizations like the Society of Financial Service Professionals, CCN, National Association of Female Executives, Alexander and Baldwin, The Internet Marketing Main Event, and many others

- Develop exclusive off-line and online business growth strategies for successful business owners — like one world-renowned surgeon who paid us more than $60,000 to keep the new media marketing strategies we developed for him a secret from anyone else in his industry for two years

- Exclusive invitations to write columns in top daily newspapers, publications like Entrepreneur Magazine®, and of course the publication of our hit book, Secrets of Online Persuasion in bookstores everywhere

- Weekly radio show guests on top network morning shows

- Reliably build a loyal subscriber list, effortlessly adding dozens of new members to our subscriber family each and every day

- Have a constant flow of new product purchases coming in day after day, week after week — without dishing out thousands per month for pay-per-click, search engine optimization, or having to buy links

- And, of course, build a million dollar business working with hundreds of entrepreneurs, small business owners, and sales professionals from around the world

All from our online marketing using exclusively new media.

What is the best advice you can give an individual or business who is considering starting a blog?

Develop and integrate your blog into a complete new media marketing strategy.

Expansion on that answer via an excerpt from our book Secrets of Online Persuasion:

Your business blog plays an important role when marketing with the New Media. To

CASE STUDY: JOHN PAUL MICEK

use it effectively, you need to know exactly how to start, maintain, and leverage your blog for ongoing benefits to your business.

For a blog to be effective, it must be well planned, well written, well organized, and well marketed. Unfortunately, we see far too many business owners stalling on the starting line and wondering why they're not getting the results they wanted.

Or they meet an obstacle on the track, and think it's over for them.

The fact is that your success with buzz, branding, connection, and profits starts with a Strategic Business Blogging Plan.

Don't just start a business blog because it's been effective in getting other people incredible results. That's not enough to sustain your efforts and get results yourself.

Establish a plan for your business blog. Link it with your complete New Media Marketing Strategy, and then integrate that with the overall marketing plan of your company.

Be unique.

Feel free to examine the blogs that contain topics and features that appeal to you. Build your own ideas from the observations of reading other blogs. Add your own unique spin as you generate ideas for your blog. Taking the time to do these things now will provide focus and direction as you move forward, starting your own blog.

What are your favorite blog development tools or applications?

Okay, here is the blatantly biased (and justifiably so) answer.

We don't suggest that business people jump into the waters of the new media marketplace using a regular old blog. We spent our first two years coaching people how to do that, and it just is not practical.

Okay, here is the blatantly biased (and justifiably so) answer.

We don't suggest that business people jump into the waters of the new media marketplace using a regular old blog. We spent our first two years coaching people how to do that, and it just is not practical.

CASE STUDY: JOHN PAUL MICEK

These are the people who fell for the hype of blog evangelists, not understanding the real story behind the technology.

The two-fold problem with all blogging software out there is simple:

1. It's built by techno-geeks for techno-geeks, not business people.

2. It's built for blogging, not to convert prospects into customers.

These techies just don't understand what it means to have to generate measurable results, increase sales, or boost profits. And they definitely don't want to be held accountable for generating those results.

The system we recommend for business people looking to make marketing with blogs and new media pushbutton easy is one we have had programmers working on for the last six-months, called BLOG i360 (**www.BLOGi360.com**).

In the simplest terms, BLOG i360 is the replacement for static old Web sites of yester-year. It is the only Web site system designed to work for you! And it is the only system that gives you ten hours of results for every one hour you put in!

BLOG i360 harnesses the profit producing power of Web 2.0, blogs, podcasts, online video, social bookmarking, and much more, and combines them into one easy to use system with one single purpose — to systematically grow your business with:

*   More traffic to your site

*   More prospects on your list

*   More dollars from sales in your pocket

BLOG i360™ makes it pushbutton easy to build your list, market, and boost sales conversions with new media. It's a system designed to grow your prospect and customer lists and increase profits. And it does it all while working for you and with the new media marketplace.

Can you name five common mistakes in blogging?

The top three mistakes business people make when they start blogging:

CASE STUDY: JOHN PAUL MICEK

Mistake #3: Focus on blogging only, instead of a complete new media marketing strategy.

Just as a weekly column in a newspaper or an attractive storefront will not grow your business on their own offline, neither will a business blog be the one tool you can use to grow your business online. A strategically balanced marketing plan using the entire new media marketplace is what is required to achieve and sustain success.

Mistake #2: Taking the word of full-time bloggers and new media evangelists as gospel.

Nothing will kill the consistency, creativity, and passion required for business people to market with blogs faster than blindly listening to the advice of people who blog full time. These are people who have decided to create jobs for themselves with their blogs. (A job and not a business because, if they stop fueling their blog, the business stops. And that is not a business at all.)

First, as a business owner and entrepreneur, your goal is to create a business entity that can profitably run without you for a month or more. Your approach to incorporating blogs and other new media channels into your online marketing efforts must be strategic and based on solid business principles

Secondly, most blogging and new media evangelists have fallen prey to the very group think that they eschew in mainstream media. They hand out advice based on rules and commandments that don't exist and needlessly hem business people in. This brings us to Mistake #1.

Mistake #1: Focusing on blogs and new media, instead of online persuasion.

Success in marketing online today is not about blogs, podcasts, social networks, or half a dozen other new media technologies. In fact, the focus on technology is why most of the marketers jumping into this new online marketplace are failing.

There's something much more important than technology that is causing this new media marketplace to grow by leaps and bounds day after day. The truth is that the foundation for the explosive growth we're seeing can be expressed in a simple three word formula presented in our book Secrets of Online Persuasion. Those three words are:

CASE STUDY: JOHN PAUL MICEK

People

Participation

Persuasion

Business owners and marketers who stay focused on these three simple words and use them as their guideposts will leave their competitors gasping for air, reaching for their oxygen masks as they try to catch up.

The reason is simple: The line between online and offline communication has blurred.

With the ever expanding evolution of interactive new media tools and the rapid adoption of broadband Internet access, offline and online interaction between people are becoming much more closely intertwined. A level of connection, trust, and rapport that was only possible through face-to-face, belly-to-belly conversations just two years ago is a reality online today.

New media technology and tools are making it possible to market effectively online. But an understanding of the mindset and motivations of today's new media consumer, combined with a mastery of online emotional influence and practical persuasion, is what makes winning loyal customers and creating raving fans a reality.

What is the relationship between your Web site and your blogs? How are they interconnected? How does the blog expand upon your Web site?

Since the best blogging systems (like WordPress® and BLOG i360) are also simple and powerful Content Management Systems, there is no longer a need to separate the blog from the Web site. They can, and should, work directly together.

This approach gives the best results for:

- Search engine optimization (attracting traffic)

- Satisfying visitors (making it easy for people to navigate when they get to your site)

- Persuading people to action (whether it be a direct purchase or taking the next step in developing a relationship with you)

CASE STUDY: JOHN PAUL MICEK

Another side benefit to this integrated approach, specifically using BLOG i360 , is that all your content (copy, audio, or video) is managed with one easy-to-use online administrative panel. No more paying Web designers every time you need a page on your site updated. And all your content is automatically indexed, organized, and easily searchable in one secure online location.

About RPM Success Group® Inc.

We formed RPM Success Group® for one simple reason: To help you stop working hard in your business, and instead, create a business that works hard for you, delivering the wealth, freedom, and lifestyle you want.

We do this by providing you access to the most cutting edge coaching and resources available. Business coaching and products to help you:

- Discover and maximize your strengths to make growing your business faster, easier, and more fun

- Get the most out of what you're currently doing to maximize profits immediately

- Expand your vision to confidently grab opportunities that will grow your business and transform your life

All to equip you to more quickly gain the freedom, fulfillment, and financial independence you want from your business.

RPM Success Group® was founded by Deborah Micek and John-Paul Micek. They're business owners and business coaches who've combined their unique (and sometimes opposing) styles to help thousands of small-business, network marketers, and sales professionals get the wealth, freedom, and lifestyle they want. And they do it all from the most remote island chain in the world!

Partners in business and life, Deborah and John-Paul live the ultimate business owner's lifestyle on the North Shore of Oahu in Hawaii where they manage their international business coaching, real estate investment, and management companies. For additional information on Deborah Micek and John Paul Micek, visit **http://www.DeborahMicek.com** and **http://www.JohnPaulMicek.com**.

CASE STUDY: JOHN PAUL MICEK

CASE STUDY: GREG RICHARDS

www.matrixwebs.com

Can you describe your introduction to blogging, how you became interested, and how has it impacted you personally?

When you're passionate about your work and/or hobbies you want to express and share your thoughts with others. Not everyone wants or even cares to hear about what you have to say, but others who share similar interests may be just as passionate about it and may actually want to read your thoughts.

I have found that online it is easy to find people who share similar interests and opinions on certain topics. For those reasons I decided to start blogging.

Over time I have really enjoyed this experience and it only makes me want to continue to do so. As long as you are interested in what you have to say others will be interested as well. People like to express themselves and blogging is a way is a therapeutic way to do so.

From a business perspective, how do you think blogging can positively impact communications, sales, and corporate image?

Blogging, whether it be business or personal, is simply a way of expression and in doing so people in return can express their logic and support. The good thing about blogging in the business world is that readers can help suggest a previously driven path and provide helpful tips to get around certain obstacles. There will always be someone who has done it before you and what better way to reach out than with a blog?

CASE STUDY: GREG RICHARDS

Customers like to know that you are a person like them. They want to know that they can relate to you and your business. Our readers, including our customers, feel more like old friends and for reasons that may seem odd to others, actually enjoy reading our thoughts and participating in the conversation.

Business blogging can only help a business to grow in ways that most might see as damaging. We have seen nothing but positive reinforcement ranging from:

*Helpful advice from our readers at a zero cost to the business

*Our customers are happy to see that we want to take time out of our schedules to share our thoughts with them

*Increased traffic flow since the launch of our employee blog section

What may seem risky to others has proven to be a brave step towards marketing and advertising. One who does not take risks will cease to expand its horizon.

What is the best advice you can give an individual or business who is considering starting a blog?

Start out by focusing on your friends, as they are the closest and most likely initial visitors. From there, try searching for other sites that blog on similar interests. Post some comments and provide a link to your blog — you want to make blog friends that will help you expand and get your name out there.

Be very expressive and passionate; this is what makes your writing interesting enough to get others to read it. You may want to consider using sites like www. pingomatic.com — a service that allows you to alert different search engines when your blog has updated.

What industry sites and blogs do you read regularly?

Typically it ranges from Web design/software development sites to motocross, biking, swimming, and fitness. I enjoy reading about hobbies that I enjoy and blogging is a good way to learn about certain locations, techniques, and is a great way to network among friends. Industry sites like **www.inwithfitness.com** and **www.yahoo.com** have really good blogs.

CASE STUDY: GREG RICHARDS

What are your favorite blog development tools or applications?

I cannot take credit for developing the blogging software we created. I have a great team of developers that did a great job on the software. Our development platform is Asp.Net using VB.

Can you name five tips for successful blogging?

- Know the purpose of your blog: Anyone at any time can create a blog, the trick is to create an online discussion that will grab the readers' attention and urge them to participate in the conversation. You want them to want to come back, to tell others about your blog, to gain support by actually listening to what others have to say. You want to be successful.

- Grab their attention: Your blog must aim to gain readers' attention. You need to create a blog of value; the content must be of something that will get people to return to see if you have posted anything new.

- Respond with comments to build relationships: A blog is a conversation so as you may assume, responding to the audience is just as important as the original post. You should work to provide new, entertaining, and informative information in order to fully capture your audience and allow it to grow. Your personal opinion along with experience will help you flourish.

- Stay on top of it: It is very easy to get careless. In order to keep things going smoothly you must be aware of each and every conversation that is in progress. It would be in one's best interest to check the blog daily as to be sure not to miss anything. There are programs that will send you e-mail notifications to track your comments and I have found this to be an important part of a blog once it has expanded.

- Don't fear criticism: Everyone has their own opinion and this goes back to grade school. Don't be afraid when others disagree or criticize your ideas; this is what makes for a good discussion. Not only will it allow you the opportunity to keep the conversation flowing, but also gives you the ability to respond with a supported reason. A lot of times people see an increase in traffic flow and can be beneficial.

Can you name five common mistakes in blogging?

CASE STUDY: GREG RICHARDS

I feel that most mistakes take place in the headline and not being able to grab the readers' attention. You want the reader to read your blog or article right now, not later.

- No Reader Benefit: No readers. The expressed benefit must be relevant and worth the time of the reader. When naming an article you should ask yourself, "What's in it for them?" or "Would I read this?" If the title doesn't tell you, then it's missing something.

- Lack of Curiosity: Engage the readers' imagination. You want your headline to be presented in a compelling fashion. If this isn't achieved, often times the reader will just move on to something else. Your headline should make you want to know what was promised or asked. Use questions, statements, challenges to compel the reader to read more.

- Lack of Specificity: Headlines that lack specificity are short on clarity, and general statements and unsupported claims are often deemed untrustworthy. Use variations of the list headline, use words like "this," "these," "here is," and "here are" to refer specifically to your content, and also use hard numbers and exact percentages when appropriate.

- Lack of Simplicity: Some headlines can be too complicated and demand too much from the reader. Saying too much can turn into a story rather than a teaser. Simplicity is a very important aspect of effective conversation when it comes to headlines. Stick to one concept, eliminate unnecessary words, and use familiar language.

- No Sense of Urgency: Some headlines make you want to read the content, but for some reason you don't. Most of the time you never get around to reading it, right? Headlines that contain the above four elements should also create a sense of urgency and prompt the reader to act immediately, but there may be a way to restate the headline that works even better. Check to see that items 1 through 4 above are truly present. If so, try reworking the headline to make it more compelling without stepping too far into hyperbole. If all else fails, examine the premise of the content itself. Is it really need to know information?

What is the best way to get a new blog promoted?

CASE STUDY: GREG RICHARDS

Syndication. Most blog readers use syndication programs to keep tabs on their favorite blog sites. It can offer a quick boost to traffic flow and readership. Blog-hosting companies, like Google's Blogger, provide syndication; it's just a matter of switching it on and adding a bit of extra code to your blog. If you're serious about expanding your audience, it's the first move to make. Other tools like Pingomatic and Digg can be used to further promote your thoughts.

What is the relationship between your Web site and your blogs? How are they interconnected? How does the blog expand upon your Web site?

We use blogs on our Web site for two reasons:

1)   Our employees like to have a platform to express ideas, or better yet solutions they have come up with. It gives them some validation in their work.

2)   To promote our company ideals.

If we happen to get more traffic because of it so much the better.

What do you think is the future of blogging?

Blogging has only just begun and will continue to grow toward new and exciting developments. There are endless possibilities for the blogging world and I am excited to see what is in store for all of us.

As a 17-year veteran of Web technology, Greg Richards uses his experience to drive Matrixwebs.com, where he serves as the President and Chief Technical Consultant. He is responsible for product development, including the creation of cutting-edge, unique, and simple-to-use technology products that enable companies to simplify running their businesses.

Matrixwebs.com, a Web technology company, was founded in 1999. Matrixwebs was ranked fourth by Silicon Valley Business Journal as a Top Ten Business in Silicon Valley in 2007. Prior to Matrixwebs, he spent 13 years at K.R. Anderson, Inc., where he was responsible for IT and software development.

Richards attended San Jose City College, is a Microsoft Certified Systems Engineer, and resides in Morgan Hill, California.

Chapter 17

Expert Opinions, Advice, & Suggestions

HOW TO AVOID BLOG BURNOUT

By Priya Shah

Blogging is a time consuming process. It involves the process of gathering, reading, digesting and compiling information into a nice, meaty post that gives your reader an insight into the unique way you see and understand issues.

Most serious business bloggers have at least two or three blogs that they write simultaneously. I have ten, but don't update all regularly.

Bloggers are also extremely passionate about what they do. Their blogs are a labor of love and they often tend to lose track of time, reading, writing and updating their blogs.

But there's only so much time in the day and only so much abuse a body can take. So how do you avoid becoming a burned-out business blogger? Here are a few tips to help keep you and your blog(s) fueled up and running for the long haul.

1. Get your priorities right

Is starting a new blog really going to help your business (or personal) objectives? If not, then don't. Simple as that. Save your energy for the tasks that help you achieve your objectives.

2. Discard the chaff

HOW TO AVOID BLOG BURNOUT

Do you have blogs that are not "hot" anymore? If you have a blog that's not getting much traffic or is about a topic that no one wants to read about anymore, give it a quiet burial.

3. Grow up

Are you continuing to blog (whether it serves your purpose or not) out of some misplaced emotional attachment to your blog? Then you probably need a 12-step program.

Lots of blogs are abandoned everyday because they stopped serving their purpose, or more often, because the bloggers just grew up and moved to greener pastures. Find more appropriate ways to spend your time or promote your business.

4. Get a life

Blogs are a poor substitute for family and friends. We bloggers tend to take our loved ones for granted because we work from home (and anywhere else we can). It's important to schedule our day to make time for family, especially when there are children around.

5. Get "un-wired"

In order to keep the ideas coming you need to do things that nurture your mind and body. Shut down your PC and get away from it for a while.

Go for a movie, take a walk in the park, work out in the gym. Get out of the house and get some fresh air. You'll be amazed at how easy (and fun) it can be it to get your creative juices flowing again.

6. Give yourself a break

If you missed blogging about something important because you had something else equally pressing to attend to, don't beat yourself up over it. Stick to a realistic blogging schedule.

Nothing is so important that it can't wait a day or two. Sometimes procrastination is not a bad thing at all. If it helps, write a bunch of posts at a time, so you can take a break and attend to other matters when you need to.

HOW TO AVOID BLOG BURNOUT

7. Quality, not quantity

Blog frequently, but not too often. Most bloggers will agree that two or three posts a week is a pretty good frequency. I usually manage to make that grade, but never push myself more than I have to.

The key is to make your posts count. Don't post about anything and everything in your field just because you have to.

Posts that are original, meaty and full of opinion are more likely to get read and linked to than posts that are just a few words with a link to the news source.

So if you're beginning to forget what your family looks like, if you think blogging is taking over your life, and your sanity, step back a bit and get things in perspective. Stop letting your blogs rule your life.

As for me, when it's a choice between the blog and the beach, the latter wins hands down.

Priya (pronounced 'pree-yaa') Florence Shah lives in a suburb of India's financial capital, Mumbai. She is an Internet publisher, marketer, entrepreneur, and full-time mom. Priya "love[s] the creative outlet and freedom [her] business offers — to be with [her] family, make a living through [her] Internet businesses, work from anywhere in the world and be [her] own boss."

Priya writes on Internet marketing, search engine optimization, business blogging, RSS technology, personal growth and spirituality, health and wellness where she helps her clients boost their Web traffic, make more profit from their Web sites and brand themselves online. Priya can be found online at http://www.priyashah.com/, http://www.marketingslave.com/ **and** http://www.soulkadee.com/.

ADVICE FOR BLOGGERS

By Justin Premick
Education Marketing Manager, AWeber Communications
http://www.aweber.com

1. Do Unto Others...

ADVICE FOR BLOGGERS

This is probably the first and most important rule in blogging just as much as anywhere else.

Part of why you start a blog is to humanize your organization, and when you do that, you (as the voice of that organization) implicitly agree to abide by the same social rules and conventions that you would as an individual.

Break those rules, and you'll pay the consequences — plenty of your readers have their own blogs, and should you treat them discourteously, the rest of the Internet will know all about it.

2. Don't Hide

This goes hand-in-hand with #1. If someone writes something bad about you, in a comment on your blog or on their own blog, don't avoid the conversation. Engage them in conversation and find out what's behind the disagreement. After all, you got into blogging to communicate, right?

If you do choose to moderate your comments (and we do here at AWeber), don't censor! If someone says something about you or your organization that you don't like, keeping it from showing up in a comment on your own blog just means it's going to appear on their blog, in detail.

That said, if someone's being abusive, there are times when it serves both of you better to talk in person, either via e-mail or phone, prior to approving or removing such a comment. The right to free speech does not guarantee the right to an audience, and if someone is intentionally trying to trash you, you're under no obligation to allow that to happen on your blog.

3. Stand For Something

Not everyone's going to agree with you or like you. If they do, they're probably bored with you.

Don't try to be everything to everyone. Know who you are (as an organization and as a person), express your viewpoints and be prepared to stand by them. If you change a stance, do it because you believe it's the right move, not because someone pressured you into it. Again, blogging imitates life here.

ADVICE FOR BLOGGERS

Being provocative is not a bad thing, especially if you're provoking a discussion among your readers. They won't all agree, but some of them will, and they'll all respect you for your frankness.

4. Publish or Perish

You don't necessarily have to say "we're going to blog every Monday, Wednesday and Friday" — but you DO need to put out content consistently. Otherwise, people will lose interest and find other places to interact. Remember, your blog is a community shared by you and your readers. Neglect that community and it will fall apart.

Located in Newtown, Pennsylvania, AWeber Communications develops and manages online opt-in e-mail newsletters, follow-up automation, and e-mail deliverability services for small business customers around the world. Customers access our Web site 24/7 to manage and send their newsletters to recipients who have specifically opted in on their Web site to receive that information.

7 QUESTIONS TO ASK YOURSELF BEFORE STARTING A BUSINESS BLOG

By Priya Shah

Blogging is the latest buzzword in online marketing and PR. But with so many marketers jumping on the blogging bandwagon, few people are giving a thought to whether blogs are really up their alley, or taking the time to consider the best ways of going about it.

If you are planning to start a business blog, ask yourself these questions before you take the final plunge.

1. Do you really need a blog?

Writing and maintaining a blog takes a certain degree of commitment, as well as a passion (or at least a liking) for stringing words into a decent sentence. If you don't enjoy writing that much, you could always create an audio or video blog.

But would your business objectives really be served by starting a blog? Or could other methods of online marketing — like SEO, ezine advertising or newsletter publishing work just as well, if not better?

7 QUESTIONS TO ASK YOURSELF BEFORE STARTING A BUSINESS BLOG

2. Whom do you want to reach with your blog?

The first step to reaching your audience is understanding where they go to find information about your products.

If your audience largely consists of people who live in your town or use products that they search for in the newspapers, offline advertising might be more suited to your purpose.

If however, your target audience belongs to one or more of these segments, a blog might be just the thing to boost your business.

- Internet users

Does your target audience really use the Internet? If not, then starting a blog (or any online activity, for that matter) will just be a huge waste of time and effort.

- Blog readers

Does your target audience read blogs? Or do they prefer to get their information in their inbox? If the latter is true, then an e-mail newsletter might be a better option than a blog.

- Search engine users

A blog is an excellent way to boost your search engine rankings and get listed for a lot of your target keywords. If you know that your audience uses search engines to find information, a blog will increase your chances of getting their attention.

3. What do you want to achieve with your blog?

There are a lot of things that a blog can do for your business. Blogs can help you:

- Increase your visibility and search engine rankings

- Brand yourself, your products, your services, your company

- Build a community and network with people who have similar interests

7 QUESTIONS TO ASK YOURSELF BEFORE STARTING A BUSINESS BLOG

- Expand your reach to those outside your current sphere of influence

- Establish your credibility as an expert or thought-leader in your field

- Put a human face on your business

- Reach out to potential customers and stakeholders

Deciding exactly what you want to achieve with your blog can help you get focused, so that you can spend your time and effort in activities that help, not hinder your business objectives.

4. How much time can you spend on your blog?

Serious business bloggers not only spend time writing their own blogs, but also spend a great deal of time reading up on current events and browsing other blogs in their field for information.

If you are prepared to put in the time and effort required to do that sort of research, your blog will serve as a good branding tool for your business.

If not, you should either hire someone to do the research or seriously rethink your decision to start a blog.

5. What blogging platform will serve your needs best?

Deciding your blogging platform is an important step that you should take only after becoming familiar with the features and benefits of each option.

The reason it is so crucial is because it can be extremely difficult to migrate an established blog to a new platform once you have started it. Moving your blog can result in you losing your data, search engine listings and readers, so don't take this decision lightly.

Decide which platform will best meet your marketing objectives, time constraints and personal preferences before you make your first post.

7 QUESTIONS TO ASK YOURSELF BEFORE STARTING A BUSINESS BLOG

According to T.L. Pakii Pierce who writes at "How to Blog for Fun & Profits!" (**http://blogforfunandprofit.blogware.com**), if you are short of time, and want to spend more time writing, then a hosted solution like Blogger, Blogware, Squarespace or Typepad might serve your purpose better.

This might also prove a better option if you want to get started as soon as possible, are new to the Internet, or are unfamiliar with scripts or code.

If, on the other hand, you're a control freak (like me) and don't mind spending some time and effort to customize your blog, then a server-installed software, like WordPress, b2Evolution or Movable Type might be just right for you.

If you don't want to install the scripts yourself, choose a hosting solution with Fantastico, which comes with a one-click install of a number of blogging software.

6. How do you plan to promote your blog?

Why is it good to know this before you start your blog? Because it will help you decide where best to invest your time and effort when you need to build traffic to your blog.

You'll learn more about the methods to promote your blog when you subscribe to the e-mail course below. Some of these tasks can be outsourced, while others you would have to do yourself.

Decide what you want to take on and look out for service providers to handle the other functions so you can start building traffic to your blog as soon as possible.

7. How will you assess the success of your blog?

To determine how successful your blog is in boosting your profile or profits you will have to measure your blog traffic and track sales or leads that have come through it.

Planning this in advance will help you take more informed decisions about your blogging metrics, choice of blogging platform and degree of customization you require on your blog.

7 QUESTIONS TO ASK YOURSELF BEFORE STARTING A BUSINESS BLOG

Understand that blogging is not for everyone. It's just another form of communication.

Don't get so hung up on the technology that you end up ignoring more appropriate ways of communicating your message.

Some things may be easier to communicate face to face, in a conference room, or even through the good old telephone.

But if you asked yourself all the questions above and decided that blogging meets all your objectives, then a blog may be just what the doctor ordered for your business.

Priya (pronounced 'pree-yaa') Florence Shah lives in a suburb of India's financial capital, Mumbai. She is internet publisher, marketer, entrepreneur and full-time mom. Priya "love the creative outlet and freedom my business offers - to be with my family, make a living through my internet businesses, work from anywhere in the world and be my own boss."

Priya writes on internet marketing, search engine optimization, business blogging, RSS technology, personal growth and spirituality, health and wellness where she helps her clients boost their web traffic, make more profit from their Web sites and brand themselves online. Priya can be found online at http://www.priyashah.com/, http://www.marketingslave.com/ **and** http://www.soulkadee.com/.

HOW TO BUILD TRAFFIC TO YOUR BLOG

By Priya Shah

With the growing interest in blogging as a means of online promotion and branding, a lot of marketers are starting blogs to promote their opinions, products, books and services. But a blog is like a Web site. "Write and they will come" isn't exactly a magic formula to bring in traffic by the boatload.

If you need to promote your Web site in order to build traffic to it, you need to promote your blog as well.

Here are some ways you can become a well-read and influential blogger.

HOW TO BUILD TRAFFIC TO YOUR BLOG

1. Write Posts That People Will Want To Read

This should be common sense, but many marketers tend to forget that their readers are real people and that you need to use the principles of online copywriting to make your headlines and copy interesting to your readers.

If you write posts that people enjoy reading, they will reward you by returning to your blog regularly.

Make your posts conversational, pithy and topical. Keep them short and stick to one topic per post.

Write often and regularly so that both readers and search engines visit your blog more often.

2. Optimize Your Posts for Search Engines

I cover this topic in detail in my article on "Search Engine Optimization For Blogs" **http://www.blog-maniac.com/blog-seo.htm**.

But here are the most important rules to follow to get your posts listed for keywords of your choice.

- Make sure your blog URL contains the primary keyword you want to optimize for

- Use your primary keywords in the title of your post

- Use your secondary keywords in the body of your post

- Use your keywords in the anchor text of links in the body of your posts

3. Submit Your Blog and RSS Feed to Directories

If you publish a blog you should submit your blog and RSS feed to big directories like Yahoo and Dmoz, as well as the numerous blog directories and search engines.

Here is the best list I've found of places to submit your feed or blog, compiled by Luigi Canali De Rossi, who writes under the pseudonym Robin Good.

HOW TO BUILD TRAFFIC TO YOUR BLOG

Best Blog Directory and RSS Submission Sites **http://www.masternewmedia.org/rss/top55/**

Another list of sites to submit your Blog: **http://www.rss-speclfications.com/rss-submission.htm**

4. Ping the Blog Services

There are a number of services designed specifically for tracking and connecting blogs. By sending a small ping to each service you let them know you've updated your blog so they can come check you out.

Bookmark the Ping-O-Matic ping results page so you can visit it and quickly ping a number of services with a single click. **http://pingomatic.com**

5. Build Links to Your Blog

I recommend the methods here as the best ways to get links pointing to your blog:

- Link to your blog from each page on your main Web site

- Trackback to other blogs in your posts

- Post legitimate comments on other blogs with related topics

- Offer to exchange links with other similarly themed blogs and Web sites

6. Edit Your Blog Posts Into Articles

One of the best methods for promoting your Web site is to write articles and submit them to article directories.

The suggestion for extending this to edit your blog posts into articles and submit them to directories came from the coach at "Explode Blog Traffic" who also has other noteworthy suggestions at his blog here: **http://bloghit.blogspot.com/2004/11/how-to-explode-blog-traffic.html**.

HOW TO BUILD TRAFFIC TO YOUR BLOG

You'll find an extensive list of article directories here: **http://www.articlewritingtips. com/submit-articles.htm**.

7. Create Buzz About Your Blog

Creating a buzz about your blog posts and topic in the local and online media will give your marketing a viral component.

- Create a controversy around your blog or it's topic.

- Distribute bumper stickers or other merchandise with your blog's URL and tagline.

- Write a press release about something newsworthy and tie it in with your blog topic.

8. Capture Subscribers by E-mail

It may seem strange for a blogger to send out updates by e-mail, but e-mail is still the #1 choice of most people who want to receive news and information.

Using a free service like Bloglet to manage your subscriptions is easy and it allows your subscribers to manage all their subscriptions from one interface. **http://www. bloglet.com**

However, if you want more control over your list and don't mind mailing out the updates yourself, you can use an autoresponder system to capture and follow-up with subscribers.

RSS responder is a new script that allows you to keep in touch and follow-up with your subscribers without the hassle of e-mail. Find it and more RSS tools here: http:// **www.rssnewssite.com**.

These tips should give you a good start to building your blog traffic.

Priya (pronounced 'pree-yaa') Florence Shah lives in a suburb of India's financial capital, Mumbai. She is internet publisher, marketer, entrepreneur and full-time

HOW TO BUILD TRAFFIC TO YOUR BLOG

mom. Priya "love the creative outlet and freedom my business offers - to be with my family, make a living through my internet businesses, work from anywhere in the world and be my own boss."

Priya writes on internet marketing, search engine optimization, business blogging, RSS technology, personal growth and spirituality, health and wellness where she helps her clients boost their web traffic, make more profit from their Web sites and brand themselves online. Priya can be found online at http://www.priyashah.com/, http://www.marketingslave.com/ and http://www.soulkadee.com/.

THE DO'S AND DON'TS OF MARKETING TO BLOGGERS

By Elise Bauer, Pacifica Group

Why is marketing to bloggers a good idea? Inbound links from blogs improves Google rank, which increases traffic from search engines. Exposure from bloggers can land a company's Web site on a social bookmarking site like Digg or Del.icio.us, driving thousands of new visitors to the site. Bloggers are perceived to be more "authentic" than traditional media, making them disproportionately influential given their size. They can also be highly targeted, engaging the very audience that a marketer might want to reach. But bloggers are a more fickle bunch than most traditional media people. Marketing to them appropriately can yield great results; approaching them the wrong way can backfire.

As someone with a well-trafficked blog and a high Google rank I get bombarded with marketing requests every day. "Your site would be great for my SEO, would you please link to it?" "You obviously love food. I would love to send you some of my ice cream for dogs and you could write about it if you wanted to." (Both real examples.) Most pitches receive a cursory glance and get deleted without a second thought. A few get a response from me, especially if the pitch is respectful and polite. Even fewer get the response the marketer was hoping for. So, what's the trick?

If you are considering reaching out to bloggers, here are a few guidelines that may help you be more effective in your approach. Note that marketing to bloggers is sort of like selling vacuums door-to-door in a neighborhood where almost everyone knows each other, and most are chatting with each other over their fences. In any strong blogging community there is a lot of back-channel talk going on. This can work to your advantage or disadvantage, depending on how you approach the bloggers in the first place. Now for the guidelines; let's start with the "Don'ts."

THE DO'S AND DON'TS OF MARKETING TO BLOGGERS

Marketing to Bloggers Don'ts

Do not send obvious form letters. Did you know that we bloggers share the form letters we receive from marketers with each other? We do. This is a great way to get nowhere with the very people you are trying to influence. It also demonstrates that you have done practically no research whatsoever on your audience. Form letters result in promoting pork sausages to vegans or pitches for ready-to-eat cheesecake filling to gourmet scratch cooks.

Do not ask for links, unless you are willing to pay for them, at which point the conversation turns to advertising policy and rates. This whole reciprocal link thing might be barely tolerable on a blogger-to-blogger level, but is considered annoying spam when it comes from a company pushing products.

Do not leave blog comments plugging your products. Talk about generating ill will! It's called blog spam. As a blogger I don't really care that you think my readers would be interested in your ready-made lemon syrup. I'm not interested in allowing a company to promote its products on my blog without my permission. If you abuse comments, eventually you'll generate such bad feelings that people will start writing in their blogs about how your company is spamming the blogosphere. Then the next time someone looks your company up in Google all they'll see is a litany of complaints. Not exactly the intended result, eh?

Do not come on too strong. If you send out product, you can follow up with a "did you receive it?" but not a "when are you going to write about it?" Do not insist on anything. And if someone doesn't want to promote your product, please don't argue with them. Thank them for their time and move on.

Do not put the blogger on your mailing list (unless they have requested it.) This should be obvious, shouldn't it? But clearly it isn't as getting put on some random marketer's e-mail newsletter or mailing list happens all the time. Bloggers hate it.

Marketing to Bloggers Do's

Start by creating a targeted list of bloggers. Use tools such as Technorati, BlogPulse, or Alexa to help find blogs that speak to your target audience. Note that although the biggest blogs may be more influential, they tend to get hit up all the time for marketing requests and may not be that responsive. So don't ignore a blog just

THE DO'S AND DON'TS OF MARKETING TO BLOGGERS

because it has 20 inbound links (as accounted for by Technorati) and not 200. It may be just the blog you want.

Know the blogs you are approaching. Before you e-mail a blogger with a pitch, read through the last two months of their posts. Really. At least that. Understand what they care about, what they write about. You'll get a much better feel for how your pitch will be received if you know who it is you are pitching to. Learn the name and gender of the blogger; it may not be immediately obvious. Address the blogger by name instead of just "Hello" or "Dear Webmaster." Check to see if the blogger has posted a review policy. Many bloggers simply will not do product reviews; you risk annoying them if they have a published policy that you have ignored.

Treat the blogger with the same respect you would a professional journalist. It's good manners. Many bloggers have a lot more influence than you would imagine, yet they are often treated as if they are inconsequential. If you treat them well, you will be rewarded in kind.

Be open to constructive feedback. If you send out a pitch and it's off the mark, most likely you will get more than a few angry e-mails back. If you are lucky, someone will take the time to offer polite, constructive feedback as to how you could reach out to bloggers more effectively. Listen to this advice. Consider it valuable consulting that you would normally have to pay thousands of dollars for and here this very nice blogger is giving it to you for free. Treat that blogger well. Assume you know nothing about marketing to bloggers, because believe me, unless you are a blogger who gets pitched all the time, you don't.

Offer to send product, no strings attached. If you have a book you're promoting, offer to send it to the blogger. Don't suggest that the blogger write a review. If she likes it enough, she might. Or she might recommend it to another blogger who ends up writing about it. Don't underestimate the social power of reciprocity. By giving a gift, if the receiver likes it, he'll likely find ways to make it up to you. This is also why some bloggers don't accept gifts or promotional product. They don't want to be indebted to anyone. So, if a blogger says no, don't take it personally.

At the end of the day it all comes down to the Golden Rule: Treat bloggers the way you would like to be treated yourself. Unlike you, the marketing professional, who probably gets paid to reach out to them, most bloggers do what they do purely for the joy of personal self expression. They pour hundreds, if not thousands of hours of their lives into their personal blogging outpost. Respect that and you might get somewhere with them.

THE DO'S AND DON'TS OF MARKETING TO BLOGGERS

Elise Bauer has advised technology companies on their business and marketing strategies for over 20 years. Elise's clients have included Apple Computer,

Symantec, Warner Music Group, Creative Labs, and a host of technology start-up companies. Elise received her MBA and BS degrees from Stanford University. In 2003, Elise created the award winning Simply Recipes (http://www.simplyrecipes.com), a food and cooking blog, which has grown to reach over 40,000 visitors a day, and produces more than three million page views per month. In February, 2007, Elise was named by the Wall Street Journal as one of the "hidden influencers" of the Web. You can find Pacifica Group online at http://www.pacifica-group.com.

STARTING A NEW BLOG? GET YOUR OWN DOMAIN NAME!

By Emily Robbins
http://www.emilyrobbins.com/how-to-blog

So, you want to start a new blog. Maybe you don't have much experience with blogging, so you don't think it's that big of a deal which platform you choose or whether you have your own domain name. Well think again.

Don't fall victim to the disaster that I landed myself in, where I started casually blogging and ended up regularly blogging and hating the platform I was using but can't easily switch because I stupidly put my blog on a subdomain of TypePad (http://blogging.typepad.com).

Now I'm at TypePad's mercy. They own my behind because they own my address — even though I'm paying $150+ a year for their service. The same could happen to you whether it's a subdomain on typepad.com, blogspot.com, or wordpress.com.

By not having your own domain name, if you ever decide to move to another blogging platform you run the risk of losing all (or a lot) of your traffic, your search engine rankings, all of your hard earned incoming links, etc. because you cannot take your URL with you.

How are you going to redirect your traffic to your new blog when you have NO ability to, say, set up a 301 Permanent Redirect? Which, for those who are wondering, would both:

  • automatically redirect human visitors to your new blog site

STARTING A NEW BLOG? GET YOUR OWN DOMAIN NAME!

- tell the search engines that your blog has permanently moved and gives it the new location

Domain names are cheap — about $9 a year for a single one, as low as $6.75 a year if you own more than 50. There is NO excuse to not have your own domain name for your blog. You will regret if at some point down the road if you don't start out with your own domain name.

www.GoDaddy.com is the site that I use to register my domain names, although there are numerous other options, such as $5.99 domain names at 1&1, and, if you only need a single domain name the cheapest option is domain names from Yahoo! for only $2.99.

The irony here is that I actually own a lot of domain names and I genuinely can't fathom why I didn't just use a domain of my own when I started my blog.

Just to clarify, my point is that you need to own your own domain name so the URL for your blog points to a domain you own and control. It's okay to use a subdomain off a domain that you own, but not one that belongs to someone else, such as that of a hosted service like typepad.com.

And it's okay to use a hosted solution — just make sure you pick one (like typepad. com or blogger.com) that allows you to use your own domain name (and always reference your blog's URL with your own domain) so that if you ever decide you want to go elsewhere, at least you'll be able to take your traffic with you. And it's also a good idea to check to see if whatever blogging platform you start with has the ability to export your posts (and comments/trackbacks) for easiest porting of your site to another platform.

Emily Robbins created her blog http://www.emilyrobbins.com/how-to-blog/ **as she journaled her quest to teach herself how to blog, including how to create blogs. It has evolved somewhat into a blogging how-to guide, with tips and tricks for both new and experienced bloggers. The site includes reviews and comparisons of various blogging platforms, her site include a comprehensive list of over 615 blogging platforms, her site includes a comprehensive list of over 615 WordPress themes to customize the look and feel of your blog, tutorials for solving specific problems, and much more.**

E-MAIL NEWSLETTERS, MAGAZINES AND BLOGS

By Meryl K. Evans

The Diva Marketing Blog commented that the newest issue of Advertising Age sounded too familiar and it wasn't just one article. It turns out the whole magazine appeared in its e-mail newsletter and discussed in blogs.

This is a challenge for businesses that diversify their marketing efforts as readers prefer to receive information in various ways: print, e-mail, feeds, Web site/blog, some of these, or all of these. The funny thing is that we at InternetVIZ have been talking about blogs and our newsletters. We discussed that if an article is ready to go before the e-mail newsletter goes out — that it might be a good idea to post it in the blog.

Our audience consists mainly of newsletter readers and that's who will most likely find the blog. Currently, I'm working on a blogging strategy, so I'll need to keep this in mind as no company wants to sound like a broken record — yet, they want to ensure their readers have the opportunity to see the information no matter how they prefer to get the information.

I read a comment somewhere that a business had no plans to start a blog because its target audience knows little or nothing about blogs. Indeed there are probably industries or groups that don't put a high priority on technology and may limit to receiving information by print or e-mail. But I believe it's rare when an industry or group shares this belief.

When I publish a new issue of a newsletter, I usually link to it from my blog along with a summary, rather than publish the whole thing. Perhaps, the best approach would be that wherever the article appears first, the second resource should provide a summary and a link to the full resource along with a note that says "From the July issue of PSJ" or "Originally posted in meryl's notes.

I agree with Toby of the Diva Marketing Blog to be careful when incorporating blogs and e-mail newsletters into a marketing plan. The marketing plan should look at all of the venues, rather than treat each venue as individual items. Of course, you can create a strategy for the blog, but also make sure you have a separate marketing strategy that looks at the big picture.

Meryl K. Evans, Content Maven behind meryl.net, has written and edited for AbsoluteWrite, ECT News Network, The Dallas Morning News, Digital Web,

E-MAIL NEWSLETTERS, MAGAZINES AND BLOGS

Lockergnome, MarketingProfs, PC Today, O'Reilly, Pearson, Sams, Wiley, and WROX. She has written copy for businesses as well as Fib-or-Not? and Meet, Mix, and Mingle games. Meryl's the author of Brilliant Outlook Pocketbooks.

Meryl writes and edits content for businesses and publications. She helps business build and maintain relationships with clients and prospects.

She is Editor-in-Chief of Shavlik's The Remediator Security Digest, a popular newsletter on computer security with over 100,000 subscribers.

She's also the editor of Professional Service Journal, an e-mail newsletter for business-to-business service providers, Intel Solution Services' Connected Digest, and TailoredMail's Focus eJournal.

Meryl is an educator with New York University's online graduate program.

She has worked for two Fortune 500 telecom companies, the U.S. federal government in Washington, D.C. and IT consulting. A native Texan, she lives a heartbeat north of Dallas in Plano, Texas with her husband and three kiddos.

WILL SPAM-BLOGGING BE THE DEATH OF BLOGGING?

By Priya Shah

Technorati reports that 30,000 to 40,000 new blogs are being created each day.

According to David Sifry, part of the growth of new blogs created each day is due to an increase in spam blogs. What are spam blogs? They are fake blogs that are created by robots in order to foster link farms, attempted search engine optimization, or drive traffic through to advertising or affiliate sites. They contain robot-generated posts made up of random words, with the title linking back to the blogger's own pages. Many bloggers see them as a way of getting their pages indexed quickly by Google and other search engines. Sifry estimates that about 20 percent of the aggregate pings Technorati receives are from spam blogs. Most of this fake blog spam comes from hosted services or from specific IP addresses.

Those in the SEO world are well aware of this. There are even services like Blogburner that encourage creation of spammy blogs and spam-pinging to get your sites

WILL SPAM-BLOGGING BE THE DEATH OF BLOGGING?

indexed quickly. As a blogging evangelist, I wholeheartedly recommend blogging as an SEO tactic. But I also emphasize that you should use your blog for more than just SEO.

At the Spam Squashing Summit, blog services decided to collaborate to report and combat blog-spamming. Technorati currently claims to catch about 90 percent of spam and remove it from the index. They also notify the blog hosting operators. But I believe that they are fighting a losing battle. As I write this there are software and robots being created that will create spam-blogs more efficiently and in ways that will be harder to detect.

The SEO "black hats" are always far ahead of the technology and safeguards that these services can put in place. Take down a few spam-blogs and hundreds more will arise. Blogging evangelist and PR guru, Steve Rubel, sums up this dilemma rather well on his Micropersuasion blog, http://www.micropersuasion.com. He believes that it is human nature for people to exploit new technologies, and that it's really up to the search engines to help put a stop to these by undercutting the economics of blogspam, much like they did with no follow and comment spam.

But the trade-off is that such a move would also reduce any impact that blogs have on search results. Fact: The more you abuse a technology, the less effective it becomes.

Spam blogging will force search engines like Google to change their ranking algorithms and eventually assign less value to links from blogs. Unless they put in safeguards to prevent robots from taking over, it is safe to assume that blogging will become less effective as an SEO tactic over time. Of course, the spammers will then just have to find new avenues and means to spam the engines.

But why ruin a good thing in the first place? Blogs are much more than just tools for search engine optimization. A blog can be a great tool for personal branding and building relationships with your Web site visitors and customers.

Instead of using blogs for spam, focus on building content-rich sites and getting high-value links to them. Don't restrict yourself to just the SEO benefits of blogging.

Appreciate the value that blogs can add to your marketing and public relations strategy and use them the way they were meant to be used.

WILL SPAM-BLOGGING BE THE DEATH OF BLOGGING?

Priya (pronounced 'pree-yaa') Florence Shah lives in a suburb of India's financial capital, Mumbai. She is internet publisher, marketer, entrepreneur and full-time mom. Priya "love the creative outlet and freedom my business offers - to be with my family, make a living through my internet businesses, work from anywhere in the world and be my own boss."

Priya writes on internet marketing, search engine optimization, business blogging, RSS technology, personal growth and spirituality, health and wellness where she helps her clients boost their web traffic, make more profit from their Web sites and brand themselves online. Priya can be found online at http://www.priyashah.com/, http://www.marketingslave.com/ and http://www.soulkadee.com/.

IT'S A BIG, BLOG WORLD OUT THERE: FIVE QUICK TIPS TO BUILDING A BETTER BLOG

By Meryl K. Evan

You know that blogs have become mainstream when they're mentioned routinely on TV, both in fiction and news programs. As recent as 18 months ago, blogs weren't discussed with everyday friends and colleagues — only with other bloggers and geeks. "Blog" today is the "e-mail" of 10 years ago: More people know about blogs, but don't necessarily use it or plan to in the future.

But the tide is turning. Technorati (**http://www.technorati.com/**) tracks millions of conversations occurring on over 30 million blogs. Blogs are not just for keeping personal diaries and sharing opinions anymore. Companies like Boeing, General Motors, and Stonyfield Farm added them to their business arsenal. It can be said that blogs are serious business.

Canadian researchers conducted a study that discovered people judge a site in one-twentieth of a second after viewing it. Literally, we decide whether or not a site appeals to us within a blink of an eye. Duh, right? Just backing up this fact with solid data.

With statistics like these, bloggers need all the help they can get to attract and keep readers. C'mon, admit it. Bloggers want readers and lots of 'em. Don't tell me that people blog for themselves — without caring about numbers. Maybe this is true for six folks, but everyone wants to be seen, adored, and admired. If we didn't, we'd blog on paper instead. Oh yeah, that's called a journal or diary.

IT'S A BIG, BLOG WORLD OUT THERE: FIVE QUICK TIPS TO BUILDING A BETTER BLOG

Starting a Blog

I wrote my first blog entry on June 1, 2000. A pitiful one that embarrasses me as I copy and paste it:

"This is my first blogger posting. I've decided to take the plunge so I can somehow keep my Web site regularly updated and embarrass myself by displaying how small my mind is compared to bloggers out there in the world like Jason Kottke or Steve Champeon. Oy, now I have to find the time to spiffy up this Web site."

If it's embarrassing, why did I put it here? Because it's online for all to find and read. I could delete it, but you know it's going to be found somewhere else like the Wayback Machine.

I had no idea what I was going to do with my blog. At the time, blogs most often focused on personal lives. However, what was written on the Web stayed on the Web even if you deleted it, and that concerned me. Much like the story of the town gossip who asked for forgiveness. The community leader advises her to get a pillow and go to the top of the hill and let the feathers out of the pillow. The gossip asks if she's forgiven, but the leader responds she is to collect all of the feathers. Of course, she returned collecting very few. "Words are like feathers. Once spoken, they're hard to gather up again."

With that in mind, I treated my blog entries as if a future manager or client would read them. Personal online information, including blogs, has become an extension of our résumés. The first time we read a blog of someone we've never met, the blogger often sounds confident and in charge. When we meet a person for the first time, that confidence doesn't always come through right away. Entering a blog compares to stepping into one's home where all the things inside reveal things about the owner.

In other words, we are more apt to be ourselves when blogging, and that's a good thing. Take me, for example. Blogging takes away the barriers of my not understanding someone else, and vice versa, due to my hearing disability. It takes away the prejudice of audism. Any barriers that get in the way of our behaving naturally are gone when we blog.

Why would anyone want to blog then, revealing so much to hundreds or thousands (if you're lucky) strangers?

IT'S A BIG, BLOG WORLD OUT THERE: FIVE QUICK TIPS TO BUILDING A BETTER BLOG

- We do it for attention.

- We do it to show off our knowledge.

- We do it to reach out to the world and feel connected.

- We do it to attract search engines so we show up higher in the search results.

Blogging is hard. It requires discipline and a thick skin. To succeed means thinking of new topics, writing about those topics, reading other blogs to join the conversations, and contributing on a regular basis. Ironically, as I wrote this, a couple of well-known bloggers have reported they're tired and thinking about quitting the blog thing. No one should be shocked. BLOGGING IS HARD.

Evolution of a Blog

I still blog after six years. In fact, I contribute to multiple blogs with three of them my own. When I first started meryl's notes blog, it had no direction and commented only on personal observations. Big whoop. I didn't lead an interesting life. I hung out with my family, worked, and volunteered. I wasn't travelling to exotic places or doing daring stunts.

About the time I started blogging, I also started freelancing on the side. The blog slowly went from, "Wow, that was some Survivor finale" to "dealing with lousy customer service" and "the challenges of being a reporter when you can't use the phone like most everyone else."

Giving Birth to More Blogs

In 2002, I started another blog when I became pregnant with kid number three (back when hearing someone say "pregnant" engendered knowing looks while saying "blog" led to puzzled-looks from people). This blog was obviously personal with a focus on pregnancy and related resources. The blog ended shortly after my little curly-haired guy arrived. (He turned three while I wrote this.) I had no desire to write about raising children — I wanted a record of what was most likely my last pregnancy.

Another blog came to life as the pregnancy-cum-baby blog ended. In preparation for an upcoming cochlear implant, I gave birth to Bionic Ear Blog. Originally, the blog

IT'S A BIG, BLOG WORLD OUT THERE: FIVE QUICK TIPS TO BUILDING A BETTER BLOG

covered the cochlear implant process and living with the implant. As the Bionic Ear Blog matured, I added entries about my life as a deaf person as I was still discovering things about being deaf after 30 years.

During this process, I learned why I blog and keep blogging. Because of my hearing, with blogs, there's no "I can't understand you" happening. I don't miss a thing when reading blogs and participating in conversations unless a blogger adds podcasts. For once, I'm not immediately judged because of my imperfect speech and inability to understand everything that's said. Really, people think you're dumb if you keep saying, "What?" and lose track of the conversation.

Together Bionic Ear Blog and meryl's notes turned into proof that I have a brain and how being deaf can make people think otherwise. I'm equal to everyone and don't feel disabled.

Blog Benefits for Businesses

Meryl's notes keeps my Web site's content fresh and attractive to search engines. Having gone full-time almost a year ago, my Web site is more important than ever as it's a marketing tool. I struggle with cold calling and in-person networking, which often lead to hang ups or looks that tell me I'm inferior (see audism). I don't rely on blogging alone — my marketing arsenal also includes e-mail newsletters, individual e-mails, instant messaging and online social networks.

Blogging won't work for everyone. In deciding what marketing avenues to pursue, businesses must evaluate blogging just like they do radio ads, newspaper ads, and direct mail. Don't let anyone tell you to start a blog because it's the coolest and latest thing. Blogs aren't a fad, but what you see today in blogs won't be there in two years. It'll be different, more integrated. MySpace has a blog tool integrated into profiles along with many other features.

Businesses can investigate discussion forums, mailing list discussion groups, wikis, blogging, e-mail newsletters, knowledge-bases, online chat, feeds (these aren't edible unless you call them "brain food"), and more. Stock exchange experts encourage diversifying. The same applies to business content and information sharing. Diversify. Some people hate getting e-mail newsletters and rather get a feed. Others don't know XML from NFL or RSS from KISS. Branching out ensures you reach people who have different preferences in how they get their information.

IT'S A BIG, BLOG WORLD OUT THERE: FIVE QUICK TIPS TO BUILDING A BETTER BLOG

Information Overkill

There is simply too much information on the Internet for the average person to access everything. Your regular rounds about the Internet amounts to dipping your toe into the Pacific Ocean. Knowing all of you are as information overloaded as I am, I set out to randomly surf thousands of blogs, covering many topics, trying to separate the good blogs from the "could-be-betters." Everyday, I scanned, glanced, and zipped through endless news, articles, blogs, and any other content my eyes could handle on my two monitors (yes, two, and I don't ever want to go back to one). I wanted to dig beneath a blog's good looks. This spontaneous experiment provided a valuable lesson of what features — content aside — make or break a blog.

You might think some of these are "duh" or "common sense ideas," but after surfing hundreds and maybe even thousands of blogs, these mistakes appeared again and again. We should be making other mistakes with our blogs, new mistakes, not these five. Here are the five tips to building a better blog —ensuring that it's the best blog possible and that you give readers what they need before they leave.

1. Small banner

If you can't see the content without scrolling, then your banner (also referred to as a header) is too big. This valuable screen estate is known as the active window or "above the fold." Your site only has a few seconds to prove itself and hiding the goods below the fold lowers your chances of getting someone to stick around.

While scrolling up and down is rarely a big deal, a reader might not want to bother scrolling when casually browsing blogs or Web sites. Why take the chance? As I surfed from blog to blog, I wanted a snapshot of the page as soon as I arrived. I'm busy. I've got sites to go to and sites to see: I'm not going to make an effort to crawl around for content. Banners are meaningless when they take up too much screen estate.

HOW TO CHECK TO SEE IF THE BANNER IS TOO BIG:

View your blog with your monitor set to 800x600. If you want to go the extra mile, check the page within a frame as seen on most blog exchange sites. With sites like About.com and blog exchanges, it's not unusual for a blog or Web site to end up in a frame, which pushes the content further down.

IT'S A BIG, BLOG WORLD OUT THERE: FIVE QUICK TIPS TO BUILDING A BETTER BLOG

WHILE WE'RE ON THE SUBJECT OF SCROLLING...

Believe it or not, horizontal scrolling happens more often than we think. Though many mice come with sideways scrolling capabilities, people complain when they come across a site with a scrollbar for right and left scrolling. Hard to believe? A search on "scrolling sideways good bad" shows few — if any —supporters and plenty of complaints.

2. Short articles

Some blogs consistently have content with over 800 words. Shoot for around 500 words or fewer. Save the longer stuff for newsletters, magazines, and other appropriate outlets. Also, use bold face type and bolded headers in the longer articles to help readers with scanning.

While the occasional long entry is okay, doing it on a regular basis doesn't impress. Instead, it drags. Readers want to read the heart of the content and get out. They don't want to spend time on a blog entry when there are thousands of blogs out there. Multiply thousands of blogs with hundreds of entries and you've got a winning recipe for information overload.

When you do post a longer than normal entry, consider posting an excerpt of the entry on the home page rather than the whole entry. If a reader wants to read more, then she can click for the rest of the article. If not, the next entry is further up the screen trying to entice the reader to stick around just a little longer.

3. Readable

Obvious? Not according to the hundreds of blogs I've visited. While bright colors may be cool to tweens and teens, they ain't cool for serious blogs. Not only are colors a problem, so is font size. How many times have you heard someone complain, "The font is too big!"? If I have to squint, then I'm not visiting again. We can use our browser's options to change the font size, but it won't work for all sites. Giving font size control to readers lets them figure out what works best for them. You may have selected a reasonable font size, but browsers, Macs versus PCs, and monitor resolution settings can shrink it. Text Sizing shows how text looks in different browsers and different PCs.

IT'S A BIG, BLOG WORLD OUT THERE: FIVE QUICK TIPS TO BUILDING A BETTER BLOG

While browsers like Firefox (which I use as my primary browser) can change text on Web sites with fonts that can't be changed, not everyone uses Firefox nor do they know how to change the text size using their browsers options.

Also, use italics sparingly. Many people have trouble reading words in italics. If you often quote resources and they're more than a paragraph long, it might be better to use quotation marks, indentation, or both.

Italics slow down reading, give us headaches, and create a difficult reading experience as we squint, drag our cursor over the content in attempt to see it better when it's selected (or copy it into word processor).

Speaking of difficult to read, a terrible trend has come to light that doesn't show signs of slowing down. I'm guilty of this with Bionic Ear because I was too lazy to change the template: Gray text on white. Gray has become the new black and stylish it's not! Stop it! Don't make me start a "GRAY Group: Gray reads awful, y'all!" Dorky, I know, but change the font to "#000000" or "black" and you won't ever hear me speak of GRAY Group again.

How to fix the font size problem. Two options:

1.   Ensure your site can be resized using the browser's resizing feature. If not, revisit the site's font settings. Check it with multiple browsers.

2.   Offer two or three size options so all the user has to do is click on an option to make the font larger or smaller.

4. Frequent

When a blog isn't regularly updated, why should people come back to it, bookmark it, or save the feed? They don't.

After all, there are many more blogs out there where the bloggers make the time to update at least two or three times a week? While a CEO of a big company might be an exception from frequent posting, it doesn't apply to most of us.

IT'S A BIG, BLOG WORLD OUT THERE: FIVE QUICK TIPS TO BUILDING A BETTER BLOG

5. Silent

Arriving on a blog and getting greeted with music can freak out the reader especially if he doesn't share the blogger's taste in music. In most cases, there is no way to turn off the music from within the site. Even if you have audio entries or podcasts, I've yet to see a blog where an audio entry started without my help.

Think about your least favorite type of music? What would you do if you hear it when you arrive on a blog?

Even though I don't have perfect hearing, unexpected music in a blog has sent me jumping out of my Aeron chair (it really works for me) a few times and not for good reason.

In addition, many surfers are in an office or other public setting as well. Not all of them have headphones plugged into the PC and get embarrassed when music starts blasting out of the blue especially if they're on a conference call or are checking a personal blog during work time (not that any of us do that!).

RECAP

Here's a recap in case you missed any of those nice tips. Build an almost perfect blog with the following ingredients in the not-so secret formula:

1. Small banner

2. Short articles

3. Readable

4. Frequent

5. Silent

I tried to make a cool abbreviation out of these by using other words and everything sucked. So this will have to do without a mnemonic.

Lagniappe — Give them more than they expect.

I try to surprise and delight my clients by adding extras. I want to do the same for you.

IT'S A BIG, BLOG WORLD OUT THERE: FIVE QUICK TIPS TO BUILDING A BETTER BLOG

While these features aren't as important, they tell new readers what your blog is about. Figuring out the blog's topic from one or two posts isn't always possible especially since most bloggers stray from their typical topics from time to time. These are tips to orient your readers and give them a better experience.

HAVE AN ABOUT PAGE

The about page doesn't have to be long. Just simply say what the site, blog, or both is about. Also telling a little about you never hurts. Sometimes I find someone's postings so fascinating that I want to know more about his or her background. Yeah, yeah, you don't like to talk about yourself because you don't want to come across as big-headed. Seriously, the information on the about page could lead to opportunities.

CHOOSE A BLOG TITLE OR USE A TAGLINE THAT SAYS WHAT THE BLOG IS ABOUT

A long time ago, I used meryl's notes in my Web site's menu. It dawned on me that Joe or Jane Smith or even my mom wouldn't know it was a blog. So I changed it to meryl's notes - blog. Since I'd been using that name for so long, I just added a tagline to overcome this rather than start with a new title.

SMILE! ADD A PHOTO

I believe having photos of people on a company Web site and blog humanizes the company because it puts a face to the faceless corporation. Unfortunately, some people choose lousy photos (referring to poses and facial expressions, not looks) that annoy more than they help. To play it safe, tuck the photo on the about page so people don't constantly see your mug every time they read your blog. A blog enjoys more eyes than the about page. Many of you will argue for posting the photo on the blog page and I can be convinced by most of those arguments. So, this one, I'll leave to your better judgement.

WHERE THE @(#)*$ ARE YOUR ARCHIVES?

I can't tell you how many times I wanted to look for older postings and spent too much time searching for archives. While most people want to read the more recent entries, occasionally we want to dig into older stuff. Of course, you've posted some wonderful stuff at a time when you had fewer readers, right? Let us discover those gems without struggling.

IT'S A BIG, BLOG WORLD OUT THERE: FIVE QUICK TIPS TO BUILDING A BETTER BLOG

BE ACCESSIBLE

Too many times when I wanted to reach the blogger, I spent 30-plus minutes searching the site for contact information. Not everyone is an A-list blogger like Robert Scoble, and his e-mail appears wide open for all to find and use. If you're overwhelmed with e-mail, create a separate one for your Web site.

Another way to be accessible is to open comments on your blog entries. Yeah, that damned comment spam made this a problem, so that's why this doesn't appear in the top five tips. Blogging applications are finding ways around spam, so when possible, open your blog to comments.

Business bloggers who shut off comments are sending a message that no one is welcome to challenge their commentary and that they're afraid to hear what the public has to say. Blog readers are smart and know when a blogger is putting on airs as opposed to being upfront and honest.

If you have great content, then the rest is easy. Just add the five tips. If you go the distance and add the extras, then you're set. If not, expect folks to click away within a blink of an eye after arriving on your blog. After all, you and I know it's a big blog world out there.

Meryl K. Evans, Content Maven behind meryl.net, has written and edited for AbsoluteWrite, ECT News Network, The Dallas Morning News, Digital Web, Lockergnome, MarketingProfs, PC Today, O'Reilly, Pearson, Sams, Wiley, and WROX. She has written copy for businesses as well as Fib-or-Not? and Meet, Mix, and Mingle games.

Meryl writes and edits content for businesses and publications. She helps business build and maintain relationships with clients and prospects.

She is Editor-in-Chief of Shavlik's The Remediator Security Digest, a popular newsletter on computer security with over 100,000 subscribers.

She's also the editor of Professional Service Journal, an e-mail newsletter for business-to-business service providers, Intel Solution Services' Connected Digest, and TailoredMail's Focus eJournal. Meryl's the author of Brilliant Outlook Pocketbooks.

IT'S A BIG, BLOG WORLD OUT THERE: FIVE QUICK TIPS TO BUILDING A BETTER BLOG

Meryl is an educator with New York University's online graduate program.

She has worked for two Fortune 500 telecom companies, the U.S. federal government in Washington, D.C. and IT consulting. A native Texan, she lives a heartbeat north of Dallas in Plano, Texas with her husband and three kiddos.

CORPORATE PRIMER ON BLOGS

By James Durbin

What Is a Blog?

A blog is a shortened version of the term Weblog, commonly referred to as an online journal, and holds one or more of the following characteristics:

1) The site is published with easy to use software, making it possible for anyone with access to a computer to publish online.

2) Blogs publish the opinion of the author, but also hyperlink back to original sources, allowing readers to form their opinions of the credibility of the author as well as the veracity of the original source.

3) Many blogs possess comment tools that allow readers to instantly publish information, opinions, and feedback.

4) Many blogs are heavily networked, using a combination of outgoing and incoming hyperlinks that connect blogs discussing similar topics. This linking increases the search engine rank and distinguishes blogs from other kinds of online communities. Blogging is experiencing explosive growth, starting with a few hundred in 2001 and reaching over 70 million by 2007, with 15 million in the U.S. (according to Technorati, a blog search engine. Each day, millions of new entries are added to the Internet. Topics cover everything from casual social and political opinions to highly expert advice on business strategies and complex scientific discussions. For every topic there are hundreds if not thousands of individuals sharing both their professional and amateur opinions.

CORPORATE PRIMER ON BLOGS

Who Is Reading These Blogs?

The majority of blogs are written by the young. The youth demographic, led by My Space, has dominated the blogging numbers and thus much of the coverage. At the same time, the expert information found in blogs by professionals has given rise to class of people called "influentials." These top 10 percent of any demographic drive public opinion from local politics to international economic opinion. Over 40 percent of the U.S. population now uses blogs to gather information, although less than 5 percent of the population writes a blog.

As blog growth grows, so does the number of readers. The first blogs focused on politics and the media. They have altered the balance of power and changed the way that large institutions package their message. Bloggers were driving forces behind the resignation of Dan Rather from CBS News and the electoral defeat of the Canadian government. As they have matured and moved into business circles, blogs have become an essential component of public expression, serving to magnify the impact of the individual experience on formerly close-mouthed organizations from Dell Computers to the U.S. Congress.

The input of millions of people, led by the elite opinion of the influentials, has the ability to drive sales (as in the case of media and entertainment), ruin marketing campaigns (product launches with poor execution or sub-par products), and soon, begin to affect company stock prices and personal reputations of company executives. The bloggers are a creative and destructive force that are just beginning to touch the business world.

Why Should a Company Start a Blog?

Companies who read blogs get first notice of breaking news, emergent trends, and the changing nature of public opinion. Company blogs executed well build credibility and project a message of self-confidence. Examples of reasons to start a corporate blog would include;

•   Employment Branding, Product Launch, Public Relations, Marketing Campaigns, Consulting Services, Vendor Relations, Media Relations, and Innovative Ideas used to established Industry Expertise.

Blogging evangelists often speak of a conversation taking place in marketplaces. Participating in the blogging world gives companies a competitive edge in that conversation. Bloggers are early adopters, expert networkers, and skilled at

CORPORATE PRIMER ON BLOGS

gathering competitive intelligence. Companies who start a blog can bring those skills in house and learn the language and etiquette of blogging, learning to engage these individuals in achieving goals. Companies that fail to engage in this conversation now will find themselves playing catch-up for years to come.

What Can Be Expected From a Successful Blogging Campaign?

1) Corporate blogs primarily are used for national branding. They allow companies to present accurate information without the filter of the media or advertising.

2) Marketing blogs can be used to amplify marketing messages through traditional channels. The use of a blog allows a company to provide a destination of information for consumers, from commercials to promotional coupons, to directions on how to use products.

3) Employment blogs allow a direct connection to online communities, increasing the number of qualified applicants by identifying communities of interest and building a loyal talent pool.

4) Public relations blogs allow a corporation to put a human touch in place of the often used "corporate-speak." From pictures of employees to CEO blogs, to instructions on how to interview, public relations blogs remind readers that your company is staffed by real people.

What Are the Potential Risks of Starting a Blog?

There are four main categories of risk:

1) There are significant negatives in your company's reputation and you aren't prepared to respond to them.

Some companies are targets for anti-company activists. If your company is in the spotlight, starting a blog about your company is not a good idea. Wal-mart, Halliburton, and anyone whose CEO is under indictment are bad candidates for blogs, because the public issues surrounding the company (whether fair or not) are going to bring readers who are interested only in embarrassing the company.

That said, there are few companies that are in that position. And even in those cases, solutions exist to use blogs to pitch a message without significant feedback. You do

CORPORATE PRIMER ON BLOGS

not have to open comments. You do not have to answer every question posed. A company blog is still under your control. To blunt or negate criticism, you need to pick topics that are related to your industry but not necessarily your company.

The goal is not to tell the world how wonderful your company is. No one will believe you. Instead, your goal is to educate the public about some facet of your industry in order to build credibility in your field. Blogs are educational tools that can help brand you with a skeptical public; they are not marketing tools that regurgitate a carefully crafted message vetted by your marketing department.

2) You don't have set guidelines in place that define what your blog is and is not.

If a company starts a blog, they should have a clear purpose and a clear statement of what they intend. Honesty is the most important factor here. Set expectations and meet them. That doesn't mean that your blogger is responsible for answering every question. An employee blogger will know nothing about marketing, and shouldn't feel obligated to discuss any issue but those they want to write about.

The blog is your communication vehicle. If you're clear what you want to write, and it's relevant to your audience, you get a pass. If you start a blog about a subject and refuse to answer tough questions directly related to that subject, that's when you're accused of falsehood and deception.

This issue will come up — but if you are prepared, you can answer the question with a simple, "That's not my area," and move on.

Having clear guidelines also protects the blogger. Firing a blogger for revealing company information is worse than never having a blog. Set clear guidelines that allow the blogger maximum freedom, and periodically review what can and cannot be discussed.

3) You're boring.

This is more important than it might first appear. A boring blog is a waste of time and money, and will bring a bigger backlash because it clearly is an attempt to tap into the power of blogging without adding to the conversation.

Outgoing links are important. No one likes a lecture, and outgoing links to new

CORPORATE PRIMER ON BLOGS

articles, studies, and other bloggers are good ways to avoid being boring. Most of all, treat the blog like you would your personal life. No one likes the person at the party who talks only about their lives and their wants. If you're going to start a blog, make it about something besides yourself.

I might sit and listen to someone discuss golf for an hour, but listening to someone tell me their golf scores for an hour isn't worth my time. For companies, this is difficult because the natural impulse is to discuss the company. Your company should make up, at most, 20 percent of the blog postings. Any more and you start sounding fake and full of yourself.

4) Comments left by readers leave the company liable to lawsuits.

One of the early concerns to corporate blogs was the threat of liability for reader comments. This danger can be entirely negated with comment moderation, which requires an approval before each comment is published. If a company prefers a more open approach, they can host the blog informally —maybe providing sponsorship to a local blogger instead of directly writing the blog. They can also list a comments policy that specifically denies liability for comments made by public commenters. Your legal department should be involved, and a corporate policy in place, but if set guidelines are in place, most legal risk can be averted (nothing's perfect).

What Examples Are There of Corporate Blogs That Have Been Successful?

Microsoft, GM, Southwest, T-Mobile, Emerson, IBM, Pfizer, Boeing, Google, Sun.... and that's off the top of my head.

Wells Fargo had a very successful corporate blog. They wrote about the San Francisco Earthquake. What does that have to do with banking, home loans, and insurance? Nothing, and everything. The blog is a public service that puts the Wells Fargo name in front of people who are curious about history (and happen to represent a great demographic to sell to). At the same time, Wells Fargo gets to talk about insurance risks without talking directly about themselves. That is a great blog.

The other companies on these lists use blogs to become thought leaders, improve public relations, discuss employment strategies, create communities of interest, and get focus group feedback on new products.

The real question is what happens when smaller companies are successful in using

CORPORATE PRIMER ON BLOGS

blogs to communicate a message. A small company with an active blog and high traffic can compete with multi-million dollar budgets of larger companies. Those are the blogs that should be studied for successful strategies.

Who Should be Responsible for Creating and Maintaining a Blog?

There is one hard and fast rule on business blogging — it has to be done by someone who enjoys what they are doing. Having an executive write a blog may seem like a good idea, but if the executive isn't fully committed and passionate, the blog will fail. Understanding how to blog and having the discipline to post regularly is a learned skill. It takes six months to a year to fully understand blogging, and so the best option is to have someone who regularly blogs either writing for you, or at least training and advising your staff until you're up and running.

This isn't rocket science, but online communities have their own etiquette, and being able to mesh firmly with your community requires some level of experience, and a willingness to make mistakes.

What Are the Costs Associated with Blogging?

You can set a blog up for $0. You can host one for $8 to $30 a month, and you can have them designed and optimized for a price range from $2,000 to $20,000.

In-house staff may or may not be qualified, but depending on the importance of your branding, blogs can be customized to your corporate identity standards.

The real cost of blogging is time. Building audience can take time, and learning to blog takes several months with a few hours a day, not just writing, but reading, commenting, and researching the information you post.

What Is the Most Important Lesson in Corporate Blogging?

The most important lesson to take away from this white paper is that blogging is a tool for communication. There are a lot of companies pitching blogs as a silver bullet for all kinds of corporate problems, and that simply isn't true.

Blogs are a tool that can be used well and used poorly. They are still in the toddler stage, especially in their uses for business. At the same time, the exponential growth in public blogging necessitates corporate involvement.

CORPORATE PRIMER ON BLOGS

In the 90s, companies were told that anyone without a Web site would be out of business in a few years. That clearly was not true, but Web sites remain important tools for business. Blogging is the same way. Thousands of companies and millions of people are experimenting with online publishing. The lessons they learn will help establish the "correct" to approach corporate blogging. Starting now has its risks, but those risks can be effectively managed with the correct corporate blogging strategy.

Durbin Media Group <http://www.durbinmedia.com>**is an interactive marketing firm based in St Louis, MO. They offer social media consulting services, online promotional campaigns and intelligence gathering for businesses interested in improving their online presence and message.**

The company blog can be found at http://www.brandstorming.com, **where two bloggers share their experience in teaching companies and individuals how and why to blog. Their clients include Fortune 500 corporations, internet start-ups, and retail businesses using blogs to complement their traditional marketing strategies. Jim Durbin, the Director of Corporate Communication, is available for speeches and presentations on individual, business, and employment blogging. jdurbin@ durbinmedia.com.**

HOW TO GET YOUR BLOG NOTICED QUICKLY AND WIDELY

By Gregory A. White

1. Submit your blog to all of the directories listed on **http://pingomatic.com/**. Pingomatic will ping 15 services all at once.

2. Ping your blog after every post at **http://pingomatic.com/**.

3. Here's a real gem: Submit your blog to **http://www.pingoat.com/**. Pingoat will ping over 50 blog ping services all at once. So you don't have to hunt for ping services and manually ping them. Pingoat pings over 50 blog ping servers (growing) with just one click.

4. Ping your blog after every post at Pingoat at **http://www.pingoat.com/**.

5. Sign up for a free account at BlogExplosion.com and register your blog there: **http://www.blogexplosion.com/**.

HOW TO GET YOUR BLOG NOTICED QUICKLY AND WIDELY

6. Submit your blog to all of the directories listed at **http://www.rss-feeds-directory. com/blog_lists.html**. (Use **http://top200-blog-rss-submit.com** to simplify the process.)

7. Sign up for a "My Yahoo" at http://my.yahoo.com/ and attach your blog to your own "My Yahoo" account. This will get your blog included in Yahoo very quickly. This is worth the effort to stop what you're doing right and do it, since Yahoo has a PR 9.

8. Use this code: **"http://add.my.yahoo.com/content?url= http://www.yourblog.com/ urblog.xml"** in your blog to allow others to put your feed on their own "My Yahoo" account.

9. Sign up for a "My MSN" at **http://www.my.msn.com/**, and attach your blog to your own "My MSN" account. This will get your blog included in MSN very quickly. This is also invaluable because MSN has a PR 8.

10. Use this code: **"http://my.msn.com/addtomymsn.armx?id= rss&ut=http://www. urblogfeedaddress.com/urblog.xml"** in your blog to allow others to put your feed on their own "My MSN" account.

11. Place the link and description of your blog in your signature, so that any posts to Forums, Outgoing E-mails, Autoresponder Courses, etc., will promote your blog.

12. Post a link and description of your blog on each of your sites.

13. Place your blog on all the major search engines. AddMe.com will submit your blog free to the top 14 search engines here:

http://www.addme.com/submission.htm.

SubmitExpress.com will submit your blog free to the top 20 Search engines here:

http://www.submitexpress.com/.

14. Use Article Directories as a resource for articles to post on your blog. Here are a few:

http://ezinearticles.com/

HOW TO GET YOUR BLOG NOTICED QUICKLY AND WIDELY

http://goarticles.com/

http://www.knowledge-finder.com/

http://www.informit.com/articles/

15. Locate blogs with a lot of traffic and place useful comments in their comment box. Be sure the blog and your comments are relevant to both your blog and theirs. Senseless posts won't help you; they'll hurt you.

16. Once you get around five to ten posts on your blog, start a PR campaign and announce it to all relevant channels.

17. Make a blog post as often as possible. More than once a day is not really necessary. Remember, if you can't write that much, go to step # 14.

Greg White, Internet Marketer, Author, Consultant and Project Manager has been running successful web projects since 2001. His sites and blogs cover Blog Marketing Tactics, Internet Marketing Tactics and a variety of 'Niche' topics, in addition to starting and marketing profitable web projects.

http://www.blogmarketingtactics.com/

http://socialbuzzmaster.com/

Glossary & Recommended Reading

Ad: For Web advertising, an ad is almost always a banner, a graphic image or set of animated images (in a file called an animated GIF) of a designated pixel size and byte size limit.

Ad impression: An ad impression, or ad view, occurs when a user pulls up a Web page through a browser and sees an ad that is served on that page.

Ad rotation: Ads are often rotated into ad spaces from a list. This is usually done automatically by software on the Web site, blog or at a central site administered by an ad broker or server facility for a network of Web sites.

Ad space: An ad space is a space on a Web page or blog that is reserved for ads. An ad space group is a group of spaces within a Web site that share the same characteristics so that an ad purchase can be made for the group of spaces.

Ad Stream: The series of advertisements viewed by the user during a single visit to a web site or blog.

Banner: A banner is an advertisement in the form of a graphic image that typically runs across a Web page or is positioned in a margin or other space reserved for ads. Banner ads are usually Graphics Interchange Format (GIF) images. Most ads are animated GIFs since animation has been shown to attract a larger percentage of user clicks. The most common larger banner ad is 468 pixels wide by 60 pixels high. Smaller sizes include 125 by 125 and 120 by 90 pixels. These and other banner sizes have been established as standard sizes by the Internet Advertising Bureau.

Aggregator: Aggregates many RSS feeds on behalf of many RSS subscribers.

Anonoblog: A blog maintained by an anonymous author.

Archives: A collection of all your posts on one page.

Atom: Atom is a machine-readable XML-based web syndication format which allows users to subscribe to blogs and other web content subject to frequent change.

Autocasting: Automated form of pod-casting that allows bloggers and blog readers to generate audio versions of text-only blogs from RSS feeds.

Audioblog: A blog where the blogger posts recordings of voice, music or other audio content.

Biz Blog: A blog owned and operated by a business.

Blacklist: Lists of URLs identified as spam URLs and therefore eliminated from comments and trackbacks on a blog.

Blammer: Blog spammer

Blaudience: The audience of a blog.

Blawg: A blog about the law.

Bleg: A blog or blog post consisting of a request to readers of the blog for ideas.

Blego: The self-worth of a blogger, as measured by the popularity of their blog (blog + ego).

Blog: Short form for weblog. A blog is a public Web site with posts or entries ordered, most often, with the most recent first. Blogs generally represent the personality of the author or reflect the purpose of the Web site that hosts the blog. It also means to maintain a blog by posting text, links, images or other content using blogging software.

Blog client: An application that allows a blogger to post, edit, format and perform a variety of functions for a blog or blogs without launching a browser.

Blog Digest: A blog whose purpose is to summarize other blogs.

Blog feed: The XML-based file into which blog hosting software embeds a machine-readable version of a blog to allow it to be syndicated for distribution, often through RSS and Atom.

Blog hopping: To jump from one blog to another.

Blog mute: Someone who only occasionally blogs.

Blog roach: A commenter who rudely disagrees with all posted content.

Blog site: The location of a blog online.

Blog Troll: A blogger who wants attention.

Blogathy: I do not want to post today and I don't care.

Blogger: a person who creates and posts to a blog.

Blogger.com: A popular blog hosting web site (free).

Blogger bash: A party for bloggers.

Bloggies: Annual blogging awards.

Blogging: The act of posting on blogs.

Blogiversary: The anniversary of a blog's founding.

Blogography: The profile section of a blog, usually containing a biography of the blogger.

Blogoholic: A blogger addicted to blogging.

Blogophobia: Fear of blogs and blogging.

Blogopotamus: A very long blog article.

Blogorrhea: An unusually high volume output of articles on a blog.

Blogosphere: The internet blogging community. The collective content of all blogs worldwide.

Blogroll: A list of blogs, usually placed in the sidebar of a blog, that reads as a list of recommendations by the blogger of other blogs.

Blogsit: To maintain a blog while the blog's original or primary author is not available (kind of like pet sitting).

Blogsite: A Web site that combines blog feeds from a number of different sources, including non-blog sources.

Blogsnob: A blogger that is unwilling to acknowledge comments on a blog from anyone outside of his or her circle of friends.

Blogspot: Hosting service for blogs operated by Blogger.com.

Blogstipation: Writer's block for bloggers.

BlogThis: Allows a blogger to blog the entry they a reading

Blogvert: A blog ad.

Blogvertising: Advertising that appears on a blog.

Blooger: Refers to a blogger acting like a teenager or in an otherwise immature or boorish manner.

Captcha: Completely Automated Public Turing test to tell Computers and Humans Apart. Those word and letter verification images you need to type in to show you are human and not a bot.

Categories: A collection of topic specific posts.

CEOBlog: A blog maintained by a chief executive officer.

Commenter: Someone who leaves a comment on a blog.

Comment Spam: Spam posted in the comment section of blogs.

Dark blog: A non-public blog.

Dashboard: When you login to your blogging account, it is the first screen with all controls, tools and functions.

Del.icio.us: The social bookmarking site where users can collectively tag favorite links.

Domain: Registered domain name.

DNQ/DNP: Do Not Quote/Do Not Print.

Expression Engine: A blog publishing software package.

Feeds: RSS/XML documents containing headlines and descriptions used for Web syndication.

Flame: To post a hostile comment, or personal attack on a blog.

Flame war: A series of flames going back and forth on a blog.

Flickr: A digital photo sharing website and web services suite.

FTP: File transfer protocol.

Google bomb: To intentionally insert words or phrases into as many blogs as possible to increase the ranking on the Google search engine.

Group blog: A blog maintained by two or more bloggers.

Harvesting: Using automated scripts known as "bots" to identify the correct syntax of email addresses on Web pages and newsgroup posts and copy the addresses to a list.

Internet: The millions of computers that are linked together around the world, allowing any computer to communicate with any other that is part of the network

Journal blog: The most common form of blog, usually taking the form of a personal diary or journal.

HTML: The language in which web pages and blogs are written and created.

Keyword: A word or phrase that a user types into a search engine when looking for specific information.

Linkbaiting: Writing good content with the sole purpose of getting it linked from multiple sites.

Link whore: Any blogger who makes an extraordinary effort to get other blogs to link his or her blog or post.

Lurker: A reader of a blog who never comments.

Metablog: To blog about blogging.

Meta tags: Hidden HTML directions for Web browsers or search engines. They include important information such as the title of each page, relevant keywords describing site content, and the description of the site that shows up when a search engine returns a search.

Milblog: A blog written by a members or veterans of any branch of the U.S. armed services.

Moblogging: A blog posted and maintained via mobile phone.

MSM: Mainstream Media

Multiblog: To create or maintain multiple blogs at the same time.

Newbie: Someone new to a discussion or blog.

Open Source: A program whose source code is made available for use or modification by other developers.

Permalink: The unique URL of a single post on a blog, used when anyone wants to link specifically to a post rather than to the most recently updated page of a blog.

Photoblog: A blog that primarily consists of photos.

Ping: Used to notify other blog tracking tools of updates, changes and trackbacks.

Plugins: Small files that add improved functionality and new features.

Plog: A personalized blog created by Amazon.com for a customer.

Podcasting: A method of distributing multimedia files (audio / videos) online using feeds for playback on mobile devices and personal computers.

Post: A single unit of content on a blog, usually consisting of at least a title and text. A blog is made up of a collection of posts.

Post scheduling: Using blogging software to write posts and schedule them for publishing in the future.

Rich media: Rich media is advertising that contains perceptual or interactive elements more elaborate than the usual banner ad. Today, the term is often used for banner ads with popup menus that let the visitor select a particular page to link to on the advertiser's site. Rich media ads are generally more challenging to create and to serve. Some early studies have shown that rich media ads tend to be more effective than ordinary animated banner ads.

RSS: Really Simple Syndication. A method of describing news or other Web content that is available for "feeding" (distribution or syndication) from an online publisher to Web users.

RSS Aggregator: Software or service that automatically check a series of RSS feeds for new items on an ongoing basis, making it possible to keep track of changes to multiple Web in real time through one application.

RSS Feed: The file that contains the latest updates to an RSS-equipped page.

RSS Publisher: A Web server that publishes RSS feeds for retrieval by aggregators and RSS readers.

RSS Reader: An application that reads many RSS feeds on behalf of one or more RSS subscriber.

RTWT: Read The Whole Thing.

Reciprocal Link: When one blogger exchanges links on its blogroll with another blogger's blogroll.

Repost: To post a comment or post that had already been posted, either within a thread or on another blog.

Search engine optimization (SEO): Making a Web site or blog more friendly to search engines, resulting in a higher page rank.

Sidebar: One or more columns generally found on the side of most blogs.

Skypecasting: The practice of using Skype, the VoIP telephony service, to create podcasts, vidcasts and blog entries.

Spambot: A program designed to collect, or harvest, e-mail addresses from the Internet in order to build mailing lists for sending unsolicited e-mail.

Sping: A ping sent from a splog to make recipients think content has been updated.

Splog: A blog composed of spam.

Syndication: The distribution a news article through an RSS or ATOM feed.

Tag: Used in blogs to identify the type or types of content that makes up a particular post.

Tag cloud: Visual representations of tags or keywords used in a blog.

Template: The blog presentation design

Thread: A series of remarks posted by people on a blog.

Thread drift: The phenomenon of off-topic posts in a thread that is devoted to a specific topic.

Trackback: A protocol that allows a blogger to link to post, often on other blogs, that relate to a selected subject. Blogging software that supports Trackback includes a "TrackBack URL" with each post that displays other blogs that have linked to it.

Trackback ping: A ping that signals a blog's server that a post on that blog has been commented upon.

Trackback spam: Sping sent by means of the Trackback system.

Vlog: A blog that contains video content.

Warblog: A blog devoted to covering an ongoing war.

Weblog: Longer, alternative form of blog. An online diary listing thoughts on a specific topic, often in reverse chronological order

Wiki: A collaborative online environment which allows contributors and readers to add to subjects, as in to en.wikipedia.org.

XML: EXtensible Markup Language. a general-purpose markup language for syndication formats used on blogs.

I recommend you build a quality reference library to assist you with your overall e-commerce online marketing portfolio, SEO and general business planning. While there are plenty of excellent books on the market, I definitely recommend you add the following to your library. All are available through Atlantic Publishing Company (**www.atlantic-pub.com**):

How to Use the Internet to Advertise, Promote and Market Your Business or Web Site — With Little or No Money

Interested in promoting your business and/or Web site, but don't have the big budget for traditional advertising? This new book will show you how to build, promote, and make money off of your Web site or brick and mortar store using the Internet, with minimal costs. Let us arm you with the knowledge you need to make your business a success! Learn how to generate more traffic for your site or store with hundreds of Internet marketing methods, including many free and low-cost promotions.

This new book presents a comprehensive, hands-on, step-by-step guide for increasing Web site traffic and traditional store traffic by using hundreds of proven tips, tools, and techniques. Learn how to target more customers to your business and optimize your

Web site from a marketing perspective. You will learn to target your campaign, use keywords, generate free advertising, search-engine strategies, learn the inside secrets of e-mail marketing, how to build Web communities, co-branding, auto-responders, Google advertising, banner advertising, eBay storefronts, Web-design information, search-engine registration, directories, and real-world examples of what strategies are succeeding and what strategies are failing. ISBN-10: 0-910627-57-6 • ISBN-13: 978-0-910627-57-3 288 Pages • Item # HIA-01 • $24.95

The Complete Guide to Google Advertising — Including Tips, Tricks, & Strategies to Create a Winning Advertising Plan

Are you one of the many who think Google is simply a search engine? Yes, it is true that Google is the most popular search engine on the Web today. More than 275 million times a day, people use Google and its related partner sites to find information on just about any subject. Many of those people are looking for your products and services. Consider this even if you don't have a Web site or product. There are tremendous opportunities on the Internet and money to be made using Google.

Google has created numerous marketing and advertising products that are fast and easy to implement in your business today including Adsense, Adwords, and the Google APIs. This new book takes the confusion and mystery out of working with Google and its various advertising and marketing programs. You will learn the secrets of working with Google — without making costly mistakes. This book is an absolute must-have for anyone who wants to succeed with advertising on Google. This book teaches you the ins and outs using all of Google's advertising and marketing tools. You will instantly start producing results and profits.

In addition to the extensive research placed in the book, we spent thousands of hours interviewing, e-mailing, and communicating with hundreds of today's most successful Google advertising experts. This book contains their secrets and proven successful ideas, including actual case studies. If you are interested in learning hundreds of hints, tricks, and secrets on how to implement effective Google marketing campaigns and ultimately earn enormous profits, then this book is for you. ISBN-10:1-60138-045-3 • ISBN-13:978-1-60138-045-6 • Item #CGA-01 • $24.95

Online Marketing Success Stories: Insider Secrets from the Experts Who Are Making Millions on the Internet Today

Standing out in the turmoil of today's Internet marketplace is a major challenge. There are many books and courses on Internet marketing; this is the only book that will provide you with insider secrets. We asked the marketing experts who make their living on the Internet every day—and they talked. Online Marketing Success Stories will give you real-life examples of how successful businesses market their products online. The information is so useful that you can read a page and put the idea into action—today!

With e-commerce expected to reach $40 billion and online businesses anticipated to increase by 500 percent through 2010, your business needs guidance from today's successful Internet marketing veterans. Learn the most efficient ways to bring consumers to your site, get visitors to purchase, how to up-sell, oversights to avoid, and how to steer clear of years of disappointment.

We spent thousands of hours interviewing, e-mailing, and communicating with hundreds of today's most successful e-commerce marketers. This book not only chronicles their achievements, but is a compilation of their secrets and proven successful ideas. If you are interested in learning hundreds of hints, tricks, and secrets on how to make money (or more money) with your Web site, then this book is for you.

Instruction is great, but advice from experts is even better, and the experts chronicled in this book are earning millions. This new exhaustively researched book will provide you with a jam-packed assortment of innovative ideas that you can put to use today. This book gives you the proven strategies, innovative ideas, and actual case studies to help you sell more with less time and effort. ISBN-10: 0-910627-65-7 • ISBN-13: 978-0-910627-65-8 288 Pages • Item # OMS-02 • $21.95

The Ultimate Guide to Search Engine Marketing: Pay Per Click Advertising Secrets Revealed

Is your ultimate goal to have more customers come to your Web site? You can increase your Web site traffic by more than 1,000 percent through the expert execution of Pay Per Click Advertising. With PPC advertising you are only drawing highly qualified visitors to your Website! PPC brings you fast results and you can reach your target audience with the most cost effective method on the Internet today.

Pay per click, or PPC, is an advertising technique that uses search engines where you can display your text ads throughout the Internet keyed to the type of business you have or the type of products you are promoting. Successful PPC advertising ensures that your text ads reach the right audience while your business only pays for the clicks your ads receive!

Master the art and science behind Pay Per Click Advertising

in a matter of hours. By investing a few dollars you can easily increase the number of visitors to your Web site and significantly increase sales! If you are looking to drive high quality, targeted traffic to your site, there is no better way than to use cost per click advertising. Since you only pay when someone actually clicks on your ad, your marketing dollars are being used more effectively and efficiently compared to any other advertising method.

The key to success in PPC advertising is to know what you are doing, devise a comprehensive and well-crafted advertising plan, and know the relationships between your Web site, search engines, and PPC advertising campaign methodology. This groundbreaking and exhaustively researched new book will provide everything you need to know to get you started on generating high-volume, high quality leads to your Web site. This new book will teach you the six steps to a successful campaign: Keyword Research, Copy Editing, Setup and Implementation, Bid Management, Performance Analysis, Return on Investment, and Reporting and Avoiding PPC Fraud.

In addition, we spent thousands of hours interviewing hundreds of today's most successful PPC masters. This book is a compilation of their secrets and proven successful ideas. Additionally, we give you hundreds of tips and tricks to ensure your Web site is optimized for maximum search engine effectiveness to drive business to your web site and increase sales and profits. In this book you will find actual case studies from companies who have used our techniques and achieved unprecedented success. If you are interested in learning hundreds of hints, tricks, and secrets on how to implement Pay Per Click advertising, optimize your Web site for maximum search engine effectiveness, develop a cost-effective marketing campaign, and ultimately earn enormous profits, then this book is for you. ISBN-10:0-910627-99-1 • ISBN-

13:978-0-910627-99-3 • Item #UGS-01 • $ 24.95

The Complete Guide to E-mail Marketing: How to Create Successful, Spam-Free Campaigns to Reach Your Target Audience and Increase Sales

Researchers estimate that by 2008 e-mail marketing revenues will surpass $1.8 billion dollars annually. Are you getting your share? According to Jupiter Research, 93 percent of U.S. Internet users consider e-mail their top online activity. E-mail is a fast, inexpensive, and highly effective way to target and address your audience. Companies like Microsoft, Amazon.com, Yahoo, as well as most Fortune 1000 firms are using responsible e-mail marketing for one simple reason. It works! And it generates profits immediately and consistently!

In this new groundbreaking book you will learn how to create top-notch e-mail marketing campaigns, how to build stronger customer relationships, generate new qualified leads and sales, learn insider secrets to build your e-mail list quickly, deal with spam filters, and the optimum days and times to send your e-mails.

In addition, we spent thousands of hours interviewing, e-mailing, and communicating with hundreds of today's most successful e-mail marketing experts. This book contains their secrets and proven successful ideas, including actual case studies. If you are interested in learning hundreds of hints, strategies, and secrets on how to implement effective e-mail marketing campaigns and ultimately earn enormous profits, then this book is for you. ISBN-10:978-1-60138-042-5 • ISBN-13:1-60138-042-9 • Item #GEM-01 • $24.95

Author Biography

Bruce C. Brown

Bruce C. Brown is an award-winning author of five books, and is active duty Coast Guard Lieutenant Commander, where he has served in a variety of assignments for nearly 24 years. Bruce is married to Vonda and has three sons: Dalton, Jordan and Colton. His books include *How to Use the Internet to Advertise, Promote and Market Your Business or Website with Little or No Money*, winner of a 2007 Independent Publisher Award, as well as *The Ultimate Guide to Search Engine Marketing: Pay Per Click Advertising Secrets*

Revealed, winner in the USA Best Books 2007 Award program. He also wrote *The Complete Guide to E-mail Marketing: How to Create Successful, Spam-Free Campaigns to Reach Your Target Audience and Increase Sales* and *The Complete Guide to Google Advertising: Including Tips, Tricks, & Strategies to Create a Winning Advertising Plan.* He is currently working on his latest project, to be published in early 2008. He has degrees from Charter Oak State College and the University of Phoenix. He currently splits his time between Land O' Lakes, Florida, and Miami, Florida.

Index